Frederick Gilbert Bourne
Forgotten Titan Of
The Gilded Age

Frederick Gilbert Bourne
Forgotten Titan Of
The Gilded Age

A BIOGRAPHY

Philip Selvaggio

ISBN: 1543014062
ISBN 13: 9781543014068

Dedication

This book is dedicated to my father Philip Selvaggio Sr. an Omaha Beach Veteran. My mother Lillian Selvaggio. My daughter Jessica. My brothers Dr. Salvatore Selvaggio DDS and Dominick Selvaggio. My sisters Jeannie Corcoran and Rosalie Kennedy.

Acknowledgments

I WOULD LIKE TO EXPRESS my gratitude to the many people who helped me to write this book!

First and foremost, I would like to thank Gina Marchese for all her time and effort and her amazing typing skills…. without her this would have taken far longer to accomplish.

The Connetquot Library, especially historian and librarian Diane Haberstroh and fellow librarian Janet Egan.

My longtime friend Richard Byne who provided photos and facts about his Great Grandfather.

The West Sayville Fire Department.

The Oakdale Historical Society.

The Suffolk County Historical Society.

Manhattan College and Librarian Amy Surak.

William Clements Library.

The New York Public Library.

Oakdale's beloved Dowling College. Reference librarian and historian Diane Holiday and Chris Kretz.

Robert and Patty Mondore whose two wonderful books on the Singer Castle are a must read.

Author June Hall McCash writer of The Jekyll Island Cottage Colony.

St. John's University in Oakdale New York.

Our Friends at Saint John's Episcopal Church in Oakdale, New York.

Howard Kroplick and the Vanderbilt Cup Race Website.

Jean Papke and the staff at the Singer Castle.

The Brooklyn Daily Eagle.

The New York Time.

The Suffolk County News.

Our Friends at Jekyll Island.

Bill Pierce.

Bobby and Helen Hennigan.

Chris Bannon.

This photograph, taken around 1913, shows Frederick Bourne and his extended family posed on the lawn of his Indian Neck Hall estate. From left to right are (first row) Anson Hard, Kenneth Bourne, Arthur K. Bourne Jr., Alfred S. Bourne Jr., and Howard D. Bourne; (second row) Florence Bourne Hard, possibly George Hard, Frederick Gilbert Bourne Hard, Barbara Bourne, and Hattie Louise Bourne; (third row) Arthur K. Bourne Sr., Ethel Hollins Bourne, George C. Bourne, Helen Cole Whitney, Marjorie Bourne, Frederick G. Bourne, Emma Keeler Bourne, Ralph B. Strassburger, May Bourne Strassburger, Alfred S. Bourne Sr., and Marion C. Bourne.

Preface

MY INTEREST IN FREDERICK BOURNE started as a youngster when I would spend many hours listening to stories about him from my elderly neighbor Lenny Sharp. From my earliest year's history has fascinated me. The stories of Mr. Bourne's wealth and generosity were indelible. For a very long time I was compelled to research the life of Mr. Bourne and recount the stories of his exploits in written form.

Several biographies were written about Mr. Bourne, all of which were articles of various lengths found in local publications. My intention was to write a definitive biography of the man and his times in book form. To bring to surface an extraordinary life which lived during extraordinary times. The dawn of the Twentieth Century and a new age of enlightenment.

My first attempt at writing this biography began in the mid 1990's. I was dismayed at the scarce amount of resource material available to me. Despite this a significant amount of resource material was found. Much of what I found was what was already written. I desired much more. It was not until data banks containing historic newspapers and books were put online that I was finally able to obtain the material needed to tell a more complete story. Hundreds of newspaper articles were written about Mr. Bourne and his family, most of which were just a few paragraphs. After two years of research involving many hundreds of hours I was able to assemble these bits of information into a cohesive story. Mr. Bourne lived a very dynamic life. He was involved in scores of projects at the same time. In the year 1903 alone he was made Commodore of the New York Yacht Club, and involved in committees associated with the America's Cup. He was amassing and driving the finest collection of automobiles, while at the same time entering his prize-winning horses in horse shows. Additionally, he was still very much involved with his business interests at the Singer Company along with his other business responsibilities. Somewhere in between he still found time to spend with his family and to be a good neighbor to his community.

With these stories overlapping in a single timeframe, I found it nearly impossible to write a biography along a single timeline that can recount these exploits in significant detail. Therefore, this book is broken down into chapters, detailing a specific interest or event in Mr. Bourne's life. Every effort was made to uncover as much information as possible to recount this story. No fictional names were used in the telling of this story. The spelling of all names is given in the form in which they were found. This biography of Mr. Frederick Bourne is the most complete extent.

Frederick Bourne, His Early Years

SEPTEMBER IS THE MOST BEAUTIFUL month in Boston. Warm ocean breezes bring a favorable temperance to the port city. Reverend George Washington Bourne knew the sea well. He served as a chaplain for the mariners working in the South Boston area. In the middle of the 19th century sea fairing was a dangerous business. Storms, war and pirating all took their toll. Sailors adopted a kindred spirit. They braved the possibility of death on every voyage and quite often met with this fate. Coming from a background of shipbuilders and sea voyagers, George Washington Bourne's calling in life and his duty to his parish was towards comforting the families whose loved ones perished on the sea.

George Washington Bourne was born in Wells, Maine on March 6, 1813. He was mostly of English decent. His uncle George Washington Bourne of Kennebunk, Maine was a well-known shipbuilder in that area. Uncle George's brother Edward wrote: "George's early tendencies were for mechanical knowledge. He wanted to know how things were done. Description would not satisfy him. He wished to see the material operations". (Page 37 Wedding Cake House) George's nephew and namesake had a different calling. A man of deep religious convictions and morality, he was not called to the sail cloth, but rather to the cloth of the Episcopalian Ministry.

Unlike Catholics, Episcopalian priests can marry. On January 24, 1843 George Washington Bourne married Harriet Gilbert of Portland Maine. Born on March 11, 1817, she was the daughter of Daniel Gilbert who was an importer of iron and steel. By 1850 thirty-seven-year-old George and his thirty-three-year-old wife Harriet were living in a modest home in South Boston on One Quincy Place. They were also the parents of three children. Six-year-old Clarice was the eldest, one-year-old Marjorie was the youngest and their only son George Jr. was two and a half years old. On Thursday morning September 17, 1850, their young son began to feel ill. At first the cough was mild, but soon the child was suffering severe nausea and the cough became more severe. By the third day the family summoned for Dr. Morris. The diagnosis was whooping cough and at the time no effective treatment was known. The symptoms became progressively worse and by the evening of September 25, 1850 the child died.

The grief-stricken family endured the burial of their only son and brother. However, the reverend and his wife had faith that God would prevail upon them another child to ease their loss. The grieving family also had to endure the brutal winter of 1851. In fact, New England would see some of the coldest weather it would ever experience during this decade. The family did endure, and by April of 1851 good news would arrive to the Bourne family. The arrival of Spring heralded the news of Harriet's pregnancy. The news of the new child brightened sprits. On December 20, 1851, the family would receive a wonderful early Christmas present, the arrival of a healthy baby boy. They named their son FREDERICK GILBERT BOURNE.

South Boston 1850

The port of South Boston was very active during the early and mid-19th century. In fact, it was growing faster than any other wards of the city. By 1855 the total population of South Boston was 15,880. South Boston was a beautiful suburban village with wide avenues and newly built residences. The owners of these residences took great pride in their lawns and gardens which were beautifully planted with fruit trees and flowers. The people of South Boston were mostly middle class, ranging in occupations from mechanics to foundry workers. There were also several yacht builders, including Elisha Harris and the Pierce Brothers. And then there was Josiah Dunham and his son, Josiah Dunham Jr. who were the only rope makers in South Boston. There was also the government ordinance testing yard where ship guns were tested before installation.

Young Frederick was immersed in this nautical environment. He often heard tales and stories of the sea which helped him develop a lifelong fascination with the subject. Like his great uncle, he exhibited an extraordinary understanding of all things mechanical. Young Frederick had a veracious thirst for knowledge. He loved reading books on history, science and adventure. He loved the power of words and was in possession of a personality that was endearing in both charm, wit and character. He was infatuated with everything, so long as it provided him the opportunity to learn. The young man also was in possession of boundless energy. It would be these characteristics that would later elevate him to the level of success that he seemed almost destined to achieve.

Frederick Bourne was not born into a life of wealth. As an Episcopalian clergyman, his father's income was modest. They had no money to send Frederick to a college. It is worthy to note that while his immediate family was poor, his mother's parents, most significantly his grandfather, was at one time in possession of some wealth as an importer of iron and steel. Just how influential this was on Mr. Bourne's immediately family is not clear. By 1860 the family had moved to New York City. Frederick Bourne was educated in the public schools of New York. His first job was with the Atlantic Submarine Wrecking Company in 1868. The company was involved with salvaging cargo from wrecked ships. His duties within the company were mostly clerical.

The job was obtained through his father's associations. Frederick was energetic, however, the company was not large enough or busy enough to satisfy his ambitions. He did gain additional knowledge in ship salvage operations which would help him later in life. The job also sharpened his organizational and clerical skills which enabled him to secure the job he would later get at the Mercantile Library.

Young Frederick Bourne was also in possession of a wonderful singing voice. As a young man, Frederick first used his singing skills as a member of the choir at Trinity Church in New York. He first joined the choir at the age of eleven in 1862.

History of Trinity Church Choir

TRINITY CHURCH HAD A LONG history dating back centuries before the arrival of Frederick Bourne. The first choirmaster was Herman von Hoboken in 1623. At that time, New York City consisted of about thirty log houses on the shore of the east river with a horse mill and two other slightly larger structures. Religious services were held until 1633 in the loft above the horse mill. In response to complaints, a small wooden church was built on Pearl Street. This was the first Church building in New York. In 1642 a substantial stone church was built measuring seventy-two feet long, fifty-two feet wide and sixteen feet high. Now the city was referred to as New Amsterdam. In 1664 New Amsterdam became New York with a population of approximately one thousand five hundred, consisting mostly of Dutch Calvinists with a small portion of French protestants and a smaller number of English settlers. However, the number of English settlers was increasing rapidly. By 1697 a charter was granted, and with the efforts of the English inhabitants, Trinity Church was built.

Trinity Church's choir during Frederick Bourne's time was progressive. The choir believed the type of music to be performed during mass should be non-traditional. Bishop Potter headed the institution during this time and probably performed Bourne's confirmation on April 5, 1863. Bourne and Bishop Potter would remain friends. Later with the help of Frederick Bourne, Bishop Potter would start the Cathedral Choir School in 1901.

Bishop Potter along with Reverend Morgan Dix fostered a prevailing belief that music should be an expression of worship, and less ecclesiastical. An increased emphasis was put on the musical tastes of their parishioners, with the hopes of heightening a feeling of exaltation within the congregation. This was a stark contrast against less-emotionally moving traditional church music. In 1866 choirmaster A.H. Messiter would lead the choir in this direction with stirring renditions of Handel's Hallelujah chorus in addition of other works by Mozart and Mendelssohn. Choirmaster Messiter notes in the introduction of his 1906 book: A History of Choir and Music of Trinity Church of New York.

"In church music, Trinity Church has been the pioneer; in early days Trinity Church was the model...the history of Trinity Church music covers the history of church music throughout the country".

Under Messiter's tutelage young Frederick along with the rest of the Trinity's Boys Choir sang these popular songs, much to the delight of the congregation. Thus, the congregation's attendance grew. Seeing this, the astute young man came to experience firsthand how to achieve success by appealing to the desire of the masses. This would be a lesson he would use very successfully later in life when spearheading the marketing campaigns at The Singer Company.

In 1870 nineteen-year-old Frederick Bourne was working as a clerk in the New York City Mercantile Library. The library was located at 17 East 47th Street between Madison and 5th Avenues in Midtown Manhattan. The library was founded in 1820. Its purpose was to provide clerks and other business professionals with an alternative to the numerous immoral activities and vices contained within the city. When not working, he spent much of his free time in the choir at Trinity Church. It was during this time that Frederick Bourne was introduced to Alfred Corning Clark.

He was an extremely energetic worker who was ambitious and willing to tackle hard jobs that other employees had pushed away. He was also not afraid to take on additional responsibility. Long hours meant nothing to him. On one afternoon when practically all the workers at The Mercantile Library had gone home, one of the executives returned for some forgotten papers and found the young man still at work and signing in a magnificent voice. The executive who noticed Mr. Bourne was Alfred Clark. After their initial meeting, Clark promised Mr. Bourne an introduction to Mr. Clark's father Edward at his house and would arrange a position with him at the Singer Company. Edward Clark was an attorney who had a prosperous practice in New York City and in his hometown of Cooperstown New York. Bourne, a quintessential erudite, impressed Mr. Clark and his guests during their discussions on world events, business and finance. Frederick Bourne's eclectic talents, personal charisma and intellect introduced him into the world of the social elite.

The Singer Legacy

THERE ARE MANY FACTORS THAT assemble the personality of Frederick Bourne. The exceptional qualities that define this man were nurtured by his early environment and the exceptional and extraordinary people who influenced him during the first twenty-four years of his life. It is more difficult to understand what factors had influenced young Frederick's interest in the pursuit of wealth, or to what lengths he would go in order to obtain it. His introduction to the Clark family is a defining factor pertaining to this point. Both Edward and Alfred Clark were astute at evaluating people. Young Frederick was not classically educated like the Clark's, however, he did possess a strong thirst for knowledge, coupled with a natural intellect and a perspicacious work ethic; qualities that both Edward and Alfred noticed and would allow the doors of opportunity to open.

Edward Clark had an adept ability to evaluate people. This quality prevailed itself best during his introduction to Isaac Singer in 1848. Unlike Clark, Singer was thoroughly immoral, boisterous, uncouth and an unscrupulous polygamist. Standing six feet four inches tall he was an imposing figure. Born in 1811, Singer grew up in abject poverty. At the age of twelve he ran away from home. He worked at unskilled jobs wherever he could find them. At the age of nineteen he secured a job in a machine shop. It was here where he discovered and developed his skills as a machinist, in addition to his creative genius. Young Isaac was involved in anything and everything that could elevate him into the limelight ranging from acting in small theaters to being involved in schemes that had the potential to make money. He would spend his hours tinkering in the machine shop. Eventually he developed a device that had the ability to carve and scroll wood. The device had title problems, and Singer needed the assistance of an attorney to allow him to file for a patent. In 1848 Singer went to Edward Clark for legal advice, and by 1849 the patent for the device was granted.

Isaac Singer

By 1850 Singer had turned his attention to perfecting a sewing machine. Sewing machines of various kinds were around since 1790 when the first one was patented in England. In 1846 Elias Howe Jr. applied for and was granted a patent for a sewing machine which was more practical than its predecessors. Howe's machine had numerous problems with it which made it difficult to be used without frequent breakdowns. It was also limited in its ability to perform many necessary functions needed to create a complete garment. Singer saw the opportunity to perfect an even more practical machine that could provide both industry and an individual with the ability to sew a cloth into a garment both quickly and efficiently. A reliable machine which would appeal to the masses.

By 1851 Singer found some financial backing and could build a proto-type. The prototype had some aspects of it that were similar to Howe's ma-chine. Once again Singer sought the legal advice of Edward Clark. Through legal negotiations Clark found a solution to Singer's problems. Isaac Singer had no money left to pay the legal expenses. He did have a product that both he and Clark believed in. Edward Clark disliked Singer's personal character-istics, but he did see that Singer possessed tireless energy towards his work. This hard-living man had a strong work ethic. Clark understood that beneath his rough exterior, Singer had the pioneering spirit of a true capitalist.

Edward Clark was conservative by nature, however, at times he was known to take a risk. He made a proposal to Singer that he would defend all of Singer's future patents and forgive his debts in return for one third owner-ship of the company that the two men decided to create. Clark bought out the investors who gave Singer the money for the earlier prototype. This left He and Singer equal partners of what eventually would become I.M. Singer and Company. Within the next twenty years the men would build the com-pany into one of the 19th centuries first multi-million dollar multi- national corporate super powers. On July 23, 1875 Isaac Singer died. Seven years later in 1882 Edward Clark also passed away. Edward's son Alfred Corning Clark inherited his father's estate which was worth upwards of fifty million dollars.

Alfred was the youngest of four children of Edward and Caroline Clark. By the time the Singer empire was well established and making millions Alfred Clark would be the only surviving heir. His brother Edward Lorraine Clark died in 1869 at the age of 31. His sister Julia died in infancy. His eldest sib-ling Ambrose was the senior Edwards' best hope of assuming the responsibili-ties of the Singer empire. In 1880 Ambrose became ill and shortly after died. After Edward Clark's death in 1882 Alfred had no choice but to assume the responsibilities of the Singer business. Alfred was reluctant to do so. His pas-sion lied in the arts. Having already gained his inheritance, Alfred's foremost desire was to pursue a life devoted to his love of music, literature and poetry.

At the time of his father's death Alfred Clark was the husband of Elizabeth Scriven Clark. The couple married in Devonshire England in October of 1869. Elizabeth was warm hearted and generous. Her generosity was best displayed by her tolerance in accepting Alfred's interests and in his need to spend a considerable amount of time from his family in pursuit of them. With Elizabeth, Alfred would have four children. All of them sons. Edward Severin, Robert, Steven and Frederick who was named after his godfather, Frederick Bourne. Alfred Clark was also the godfather to Frederick Bourne's son Alfred Severin Bourne.

In his book the Clarke's of Cooperstown, author Nicholas Fox Weber surmises that Alfred Corning Clark was "a man of consuming passion and refine sensibility" was in actuality living a double life. In true Victorian fashion Clark presented himself as a devoted husband, father and church goer. A wealthy man who without a career in the traditional sense, was both generous and modest. Although without a traditional career, Arthur was far from being an idler. He was perceived by many as a book worm. A man who for hours could pour over books and manuscripts absorbing their content. He took command of several languages including French, German and Norwegian. Alfred would master the Norwegian language through his relationship with a Norwegian tenor named Lorentz Severin Skougaard. Edward Clark heard Skougaard sing in Paris where he was a pupil of the celebrated Panotka school of opera. In 1866 he offered the 29-year-old singer the chance to perform in the United States. Edward Clark funded the trip back to the United States for Skougaard. After his arrival, he was scheduled to perform in New York City. However, during that year there was a cholera epidemic plaguing the city. The family allowed Skougaard to stay with them at their home in Cooperstown New York. It was there that Skougaard met Alfred Clark. Throughout the late summer the two men spent many hours together sailing, rowing and hiking together and the friendship was bonded.

By late October the epidemic in Manhattan had subsided. On the 27th of October, 1866 Skougaard, who now took on the professional name Severini gave his first performance in the opera La Sonnaambula (The Sleepwalker) written by Vincenzo Bellini. He also performed renditions of arias by Verdi and Rossini to mixed reviews. Some critics considered his voice to be too delicate. In an article of The American Art Journal, dated October of 1866, a critic defends Severini by explaining that the role he played as Elvino is one of youth and innocence. To sing the role in a strong voice would "*be against those delicate conceptions of.... Bellinni. We shall always cry, bravo, bravo! to Severini who...knows how to give us our music as it ought to be given and thus make our nation proud of him, though he is a stranger.*" After the New York performance Skougaard returned to Norway. He worked on perfecting his singing back in Europe and would return to New York once a year to perform. He would always stay with the Clark's either in Cooperstown or in Manhattan.

While in Cooperstown Severini also performed with Mrs. Emily Doubleday, the organist at the Episcopalian Christ Church. In a concert held there, Severini sang in four different languages. The song from Gumbert, "Ye Merry Birds" was rendered in German. The "Standard Watch" in English. A song from Lucia in Italian and "Gounod's Serenade" in French. It was feared that the local audience would fail to understand and appreciate the renditions, however, the audience was delighted and enthusiastic. In a September 21, 1867 article in The Watson's Art Journal, a critic states: "Signor Severini belongs to the class of singers popularly called light tenors in distinction from the robusto or heavy tenor. He is a finished artiste, and his voice is especially brilliant and flexible in the upper notes. The audience seemed uncertain which to admire most, The Signor's singing or the quiet grace and ease of his being which indicate at once the confident artiste and the thoroughbred gentleman".

Later Alfred Clark spoke to Severini about his desire to create an institution for young men with singing talent. A place where promising voices could develop their singing talents under the tutelage and supervision of professional instructors. Severini fell in with the idea immediately. In 1875 Clark purchased two houses at 64 and 66 West 22nd Street in Manhattan, directly down the block from his own home at number 7. The home at number 66 would be for Severini, the other house would be fitted with the instruments and furnishings necessary for the fledgling singers. Rich or poor any man with singing potential was given the chance to improve his talent. Mr. Clark would frequently come by to hear them sing. On these occasions, he made himself as inconspicuous as possible and if introduced was done so as a friend of Mr. Severini.

Lorentz Severin Skougaard

In 1866 Skougaard took on the professional name Severini. Along with Alfred Clark, Severini created an institution for young men with singing talent. After sometime a group of particularly talented singers became quite good. Eventually these singers would join with others singers in the Mendelssohn Glee Club.

The two adjacent homes illustrated were purchased by Mr. Clark in 1875. The houses were located at 64 and 66 West 22nd Street. It was the home of Lorentz Severin Skougaard (Severini) and the location of the Glee Club.

After some time, a group of particularly talented singers were becoming quite good. At Mr. Clark's suggestion Mr. Severini was prompted to organize a glee club among his pupils. Eventually these singers would join with other singers in the Mendelssohn Glee Club. It was during this time that Frederick Bourne would strengthen his friendship with both Alfred Clark and with Severini. In February of 1885 Skougaard Severini died. At his bedside was Alfred Clark, Frederick Bourne and Skougaard's brother Jens. Funeral services were held in the Church of Incarnation on Madison Avenue near 35th Street; the parish where Mr. Clark and Mr. Bourne belonged. Frederick Bourne was one of the pallbearers. Music for the services were performed by a male quartet composed of Severini's pupils. Also performing were Miss Kate Percy Douglass, Soprano. Miss Douglass sang "Angles Ever Bright and Fair". Clark was strongly moved by the rendition and was deeply saddened by the loss of his friend and partner. Days after the funeral services members of the Mendelssohn Glee Club along with other friends and associates received diamond rings and stick pins from an "anonymous" benefactor on behalf of Mr. Severini. A life annuity of $600.00 per year was also provided for each person.

There is more than substantial evidence that Alfred Corning Clark was living a dual life between his marriage and his relationship with Severini. However, there is no evidence that his involvement with any of the singers in his organization or with Mr. Bourne was anything more than plutonic. He was appreciative of the artistic and emotional expression of the human voice and its ability to move people to a state of exultation and grace. He enjoyed the sound of coral music from a distance in every sense.

The Bourne and Clark Friendship

OVER A PERIOD OF TIME the friendship between Bourne and Alfred Clark became close. Eventually the young man would be trusted to handle business matters within the company as well as matters associated with the estate of Edward Clark after his death. Bourne would eventually secure a position in the company as a stenographer. This position allowed him to sit in on company board meetings. As their friendship grew a feeling of mutual trust and respect was developed between the two men. Bourne continued to impress Mr. Clark with his business savvy. Alfred promoted Bourne to more responsible positions and would frequently ask the young man to attend board meetings on his behalf.

It was during his early years working for Singer that Frederick Bourne met his wife to be. Her name was Emily (Emma) Keeler. She was born on April 10, 1855. The Keeler's belong to an old New York and Connecticut family and were of Scottish and English decent. Her grandfather was J.E. Davidson, a noted yachtsman. She was also the great granddaughter of David Whitney who was a master mariner in Norwalk Connecticut. Tradition says that he was a soldier in the Revolutionary War. On February 9, 1875 Mr. Bourne married Emma Keeler. By January of the following year Mrs. Bourne would give birth to their first child Frederick Bourne Jr. On October 7, 1877, their second son Arthur was born. Their daughter May was born on April 7, 1881. According to Greenwood Cemetery records Marion was born on June 4, 1883. Grave records show Alfred Severin

Bourne's date of birth as August 3, 1883. During these early years, the young family would make yearly trips to Cooperstown where they would sojourn on the shores of Otsego Lake. Here the family would indulge in some of their earliest yachting excursions.

It was during one of these trips on July 13, 1884 where a tragic event took place. While in Cooperstown the couple's eldest child Frederick Jr. passed away at the age of 8 years and 6 months old. The exact circumstances of the child's death are unclear. The boy's body was brought back to New York City where the funeral took place. Internment was at Greenwood Cemetery. The couple also had a daughter named Louisa who was born in 1879 and apparently died in 1884. The circumstances of both her and her brother's death are unclear. In what was a tragic twist of irony, Mr. Bourne's eldest son and namesake died in childhood. It was the same fate his eldest brother of his father's namesake also endured. The poet Walt Whitman wrote "I mourn'd and yet shall mourn with every returning Spring". The following year in 1885 they would greet the birth of another child, a daughter they would name Helen. The next year on January 6, 1886 their daughter Florence was born. The happiness of the births of their daughters was all too brief for on January 22, 1887 two-year-old Helen would also die due to an illness. The following year in 1888 George Gault Bourne was born, then Marjorie on May 5, 1890, Kenneth in 1891 and the families youngest child Howard Davidson Bourne on April 12, 1893.

Somewhere between the elation of the birth of his children and the sadness of losing three of his young ones in the 1880's, Mr. Bourne always managed to spend time with his wife and family. This tireless man was also the prevayer of great love and sympathy. He was unselfish and made good use of his time. His children showed him a great deal of love and affection; always referring to him as "Daddy".

Alfred Severin Bourne

Alfred Severin Bourne was the Godson of Alfred Corning Clark. After Clark's death in 1896, Alfred inherited $1Million dollars on his 21st birthday in 1904. Alfred later went on to become a champion Golfer, and good friend of legendary Golfer Bobby Jones. Alfred was instrumental in starting the Augusta National Golf Club in Augusta Georgia, home of The Masters Tournament.

Frederick Bourne The Athlete

IT WAS THE SUMMER OF 1913 on a warm Friday during the July 4th week-end. The place was the auditorium at St. Lawrence Roman Catholic Church in Sayville, New York. The event was an exhibition of "Scientific Boxing" given by the Sayville Athletic Club and was supervised and managed by the Reverend Michael P. Heffernan, the rector of the church. Visiting boxers from the New York Athletic Club were put up against Sayville's best for four round boxing matches.

In charge of the New York Athletic Club pugilists was Mike Donovan, a famous retired fighter and former middle-weight champion. He also served for many years as an instructor for the club. When a news reporter was introduced to Mr. Donovan Mike inquired *"How is Fred Bourne? Lives somewhere around here, doesn't he? He was the fastest amateur heavyweight I ever saw. He was my star pupil and I was proud of him"*. Mr. Donovan was not exaggerating. Among his other attributes, Frederick Bourne was also an outstanding athlete standing 5' 10 ½" tall with broad shoulders. However, later in life the commodore enjoyed the pleasures of fine cigars and cigarette smoking which ultimately contributed to the deterioration of his health.

Mike Donovan
WORLD'S CHAMPION IN THE SIXTIES

Pugilist Mike Donovan trained
Frederick Bourne for a boxing match
with John L. Sullivan.

In the late 1870's and well into the 1890's the sport of boxing experienced a popular revival amongst men of wealth or with distinguished backgrounds as a pastime and as a form of healthy exercise. In the boxing ring Mr. Bourne, would earn further respect amongst his peers exhibiting fortitude, strength and courage. It can be speculated that his participation in boxing at this time could be in response to dispel any gossip about his Glee Club activities. Mr. Bourne became a member of the New York Athletic Club in the early 1880's. During this time, Mike Donovan would host amateur boxing events where he would often pit his finest pupils against some of the best professional boxers of the time.

On March 9, 1884 Donovan set up a four-round spar with his star pupil Frederick Bourne against the legendary boxer John L. Sullivan. Donovan had gotten Fred into fine shape for the exhibition which was presented at Tammany Hall in New York City. Donovan claimed that the young man *"made a great hit and I believe the old Jawn (Sullivan) was a bit surprised".* There is no doubt that Mr. Bourne put his all into the event and undoubtedly took some substantial blows to the body as Mr. Sullivan was accustom to doing. In later years Mr. Bourne suffered frequently from gastro intestinal illnesses. It is entirely possible that Mr. Bourne's later afflictions may have been either directly or indirectly caused by internal organ injury suffered during his experiences in the boxing ring.

During the 1880's Frederick Bourne was also involved with cycling and was a member of the Citizens Bicycle Club. In July of 1885 in Buffalo, New York Mr. Bourne was the commander of the Citizens Bicycle Clubs participation in a cycling event taking place in that city. Thousands of bicyclists arrived by train from all over the country. Frederick also enjoyed cycling as a leisure activity and was frequently seen on the streets of New York City riding his bicycle from his new apartment at the Dakotas to his office at Singer. Throughout his life, Frederick Bourne was an avid athlete and participated in a variety of sports from swimming, shooting, bowling, horseback riding among many others.

George Henry Macy, *left*, on a hunting party at Jekyll Island. (Courtesy of William Kingsland Macy Jr.)

Pictured here fourth on the right. Mr. Bourne was an avid sportsman of the outdoors. Before golf grew in its popularity, hunting was the preferred sport of the wealthy businessman. Mr. Bourne was also a member of the SPCA. Courtesy William Kingsland Macy Jr. and June Hall McCash.

The Dakota Apartments

AFTER THEIR MARRIAGE, THE BOURNE's first New York City's address was 134 East 66th Street. The house was three blocks away from the entrance to Central Park off 5th Avenue. The Bourne family was growing rapidly. In conjunction with the expansion of his family, Mr. Bourne's responsibilities with Singer was also growing. One of these duties was his involvement with the design of the interior decorations and furnishings on the first floor of the new apartment building the Clark family was building on 72nd Street. The complex was one of the first truly luxury apartment houses in the city. Apartment living, until this time, was mostly reserved for families on the lower part of the economic and sociological scale. Apartments were mostly tenement dwellings reserved for poorer people in a lower class. This was the prevailing view in America, however in Europe this was not the case. Both Mr. Clark and Mr. Bourne had traveled to Europe on several occasions by this time and had fostered a new concept of apartment living for the future of the city which would eventually be the catalyst for the construction of the new building.

Edward Clark broke ground on the Dakota's construction in 1880 with a budget of $1,000,000, an unprecedented amount for the times. One of Mr. Clark's friends remarked with some sarcasm that putting up a building so far north and so far west within the city was akin to building it in Dakota (at that time the Dakota territory was not yet entered into statehood.) Clark rather enjoyed the metaphor and instructed the architect, Henry Hardenbergh, to include details within the building's interior and exterior design illustrating an American West motif. These included:

arrowheads, ears of corn and stalks of wheat. Above the buildings main portico could be found an Indian head carved in stone in base relief and is still enjoyed as one of the buildings trademarks. Originally the name of the building was to be called the Clark Apartments. In time the nickname caught on and soon after its construction the building was known as the Dakota Flats and eventually just The Dakota.

By the middle of the 1880's Alfred Clark was paying close attention to the construction of the Dakota complex and his protégé Frederick Bourne. Clark saw the Bourne family was growing rapidly. One day he sent for Mr. Bourne and explained his intentions on getting the young man involved in the project. He was interested in getting Bourne to design the first floor of the building. Upon their meeting, Mr. Clark said *"I want you to give it your most particular attention. Arrange the plans and decorations just as though you were going to occupy it (yourself.) Let there be nothing lacking to make it a model of comfort and convenience. When the building is completed, furnish it according to your own ideas. Never mind about the expense".*

Bourne threw himself into the project with great enthusiasm as he did with all things. To help with the details Mr. Bourne assigned many of the projects work to his wife Emma who in fact can be credited with its final outcome. After the completion of the interior decoration, Mr. Bourne invited Mr. Clark to the portion of the flat they designed and decorated. After inspection, Mr. Clark exclaimed his appreciation and approval and said *"It is very good. I like it immensely".* In a surprise move Clark gifted the entire first floor of the flat for the Bourne family to move into.

Over the years' the apartment building would become the home of numerous movie stars and celebrities including John Lennon. On December 8, 1980 the Dakota complex gained worldwide attention as the site where Lennon was tragically murdered, silencing the voice of one of the most inspirational and creative geniuses of our time.

By1889 Alfred Clark was very pleased with Frederick Bourne's management of the business affairs of the Singer Company. He knew he had made a wise choice in selecting Frederick for the position. Alfred had inherited from his father the ability to judge good character and in Frederick Bourne his judgement was entirely correct. When Bourne assumed power within the company as its Chief Executive Officer the company had produced a total of 13,250,000 machines since its inception in 1853. When Bourne took charge much of the machines – over 50% were produced by the company's foreign market facilities. The Singer Sewing Machine was the first product to achieve such success within foreign markets. Under Frederick Bourne's leadership the company would lay inroads on the improvement and development of its sales department. One enormously popular sales device was the creation and distribution of beautifully illustrated novelty items such as photo cards and calendars. The items were extremely popular and succeeded in making the Singer name the first to come to mind when thinking of sewing machines. For decades, the Singer sewing machine would become the most valuable possession in the household.

The Singer machine developed and emerging cottage industry for woman. They created new designs and fashions for the clothing industries. By the 1890's, the cumbersome dress bustle was fully abandoned and lighter weight underwear was designed and worn. Women were instrumental in creating these new designs. With the money earned, they were able to live on their own. All of these factors played into the eventual liberation of women enabling them to enter the mainstream of world finance and culture.

Frederick Bourne also believed in keeping the sewing machine on the cutting edge of technology. He did this by creating a research and development department which helped in designing new innovations on the performance and durability of the Singer product. The introduction of new models of sewing machines to its line included several machines designed specifically for the household. The models included the class 13, 15, and 27. The machines quickly became popular for its ease of use and durability. The Singer machines were also housed in well-crafted wood cabinets which allowed the machine to compliment the furnishings of any home.

"In 1895 Frederick Bourne noted the company produced about 694,000 sewing machine Cabinets annually. At one time, the Singer Company supported the largest woodworking factories in the world in

Arkansas, Illinois and South Bend Indiana" (Page 119 Bissell: First Conglomerate).

The most promising emerging markets for the Singer machines were in Southern and Eastern Europe. With the help of his European agent, George Neidlinger, the Singer company began manufacturing machines in Russia. On April 23, 1897 Frederick Bourne boarded the steamer Teutonic. His destination was St. Petersburg and then Moscow where he would oversee the new manufacturing facility which was to be located in St. Petersburg. He would remain there for several months. The operation in Russia was a huge success. By 1902 the "Kompaniya Singer" as it came to be known there, was growing rapidly in size. Its sales climbed into the hundreds of thousands. In St. Petersburg, Bourne would build a new six story headquarters. The structure would be historically significant for the fact that it was the first building in Russia constructed with steel girders. The February 28, 1902 edition of the New York Times reported the Singer Company manufactured over 1,200,000 machines and 100,000,000 needles worldwide.

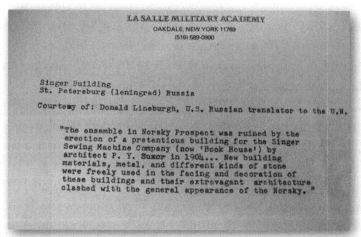

The Singer facility built in Russia was a groundbreaking achievement in architecture for the area. However, as the above letter documents, the Russian government and many of its people had mixed opinions regarding its design. Photo compliments of Manhattan College.

The Singer Tower

HALFWAY THROUGH THE FIRST DECADE of the 20th century Frederick Bourne's salary within the Singer Company was more than $1,000,000 a year. By 1905 the 54-year-old President would step down from his position in the company. However, he would remain an active director and consultant within the company until his death. Bourne also maintained other business interests including owning shares in the Atlas Portland Cement Company, Directors in the Bank of Manhattan Company, the Knickerbocker Trust Company and the Central Railroad of New Jersey and Long Island Railroad Company. Frederick Bourne would secure a contract for the Atlas Portland Cement Company for one of its largest building projects located in Manhattan. Bourne was a consultant for the construction of the company's new tower located at the corner of Broadway and Liberty Street in New York. The Singer Tower, as it would come to be known would be the tallest building ever constructed. Plans for the tower were filed on June 29, 1906. The architect would be Earnest Flagg.

Initially the project was called by Flagg "The Bourne Building Edition." The tower would rise above two existing structures: the Singer building and the Bourne building. The new building would unite into one structure. To do this it was necessary to alter the original Singer and Bourne buildings internally and carry connecting corridors from the new tower located on Broadway, through the old buildings to the Bourne building at the other end on Liberty Street. Plans for the tower would elevate it to 47 stories at a height of 612 feet, making it the tallest building in the world. Later plans allowed for the edition of 4 stories to the existing Singer and Bourne buildings. This edition would allow for easier access to the upper levels of the tower. The work of raising the floor levels on the Singer and Bourne buildings would be known as the "Singer Building Extension."

Plans for the tower and the extension were passed on September 12, 1906. Not long after, work commenced on the buildings construction. Steam lines were extended from the existing building for operation of air compressors which were utilized for the construction of the foundation caissons. On September 24th excavations were started. On October 1st materials for the first caissons were delivered, and on October 25th pouring of Atlas Concrete would begin. Construction of the tallest building in the world had begun.

Earnest Flagg's plans for the design of the tower would embrace his belief that "a thing of beauty is a joy forever." The Singer Tower would emerge from the city streets like a fledgling redwood rising in a forest. Flagg understood the speculative, ever upward growth of Manhattan was a reality. He was a pioneer in the belief that much consideration should be given to the effect large buildings would have on their neighboring structures. He went on to criticize that such buildings would restrict sunlight and panoramic views of the horizon on behalf of smaller buildings. With this in mind Flagg's plan for the tower would be that of a setback design. His solution to the problem of restricted vertical space was to allow the lower portion of the building to cover the entire lot. The construction of the remaining structure, that being its tower, would be restricted to approximately 25% of the size of its base. The Singer Tower with its set back design would allow a concentration of vertical space with minimal interference with light and air to adjoining property. Flagg went on the become an advocate of skyscraper legislation. In 1916 a city zoning law was passed which incorporated some of Flagg's beliefs. It also favored a less drastic step back design policy which was to be a more favorable solution for future skyscrapers.

A large force of skilled engineers and laborers were hired for the buildings construction. Careful preparations were made with an emphasis put on safety by Mr. Bourne. It must be noted that not a single worker was seriously injured or killed during the construction of the Singer Tower. While the tower was being built hundreds of spectators would line the streets daily and marvel as the towers girders were set into place. Newspapers gave much publicity to the construction and on the exotic materials that would be used in its interior and exterior ornamentation.

Ornamental ironwork was made and erected by the Whale Creek Iron Works Company. Railings of wrought iron with scroll designs graced the front of the building. Mr. Bourne's experience with fire loss caused him to put an emphasis on fireproofing the Singer Tower. Many surface areas were protected with a covering of terracotta tile. Fireproofing was also included in the construction of the flooring and was included in between the spans of the steel floor beams.

The handsome brick face of the tower was furnished by the John B. Rose Company of West 52nd Street New York. Over 1,000,000 red bricks were used in the towers construction. One of the bricks at the top of the tower was made of silver instead of clay to emphasize the fact that it was the highest brick in the world. Another more interesting, as well as record setting feature of the Singer Tower was the elevator systems installed. The tower had a total of nine elevators. The system was installed by the Otis Elevator Company. One of the traction elevators ascended from the ground floor to the 40th floor-584 feet. This distance was covered without changing cars. It was the first elevator ever installed for service to cover such a height. It was important because it exemplified an ideal, the potential of elevators for future use.

Upon its completion, on May 1, 1908, the Singer Tower would be one of the most elegant buildings every constructed. Upon entering its main corridor visitors were delighted with its massive marble piers, and the details of the decorations located in the lobby. Each pier was faced with Italian Pavonazzo marble-the finest and most beautiful marble in the world and set in a frame of silver gray Montarenti Sienna Marble, with corners trimmed with beaded bronze. Additional wall decorations included needle and thread imagery. Equally striking was the exterior with its bulbous mansard and giant lantern at its peak. The Singer Tower would be one of the most iconic structures in the New York skyline.

*Postcard depicting Singer Tower soon
after its completion*

*This photograph is of the Singer Tower's interior.
Photograph depicts ornamentation and exotic marbles
which were used throughout the interior of the structure.*

Frederick Bourne and his architect Earnest Flagg had succeeded in creating what they believed was a record setting and innovative masterpiece in modern skyscraper design. However, the Singer Tower did not hold the title of tallest building in the world for long. In 1909 it was surpassed by the Metropolitan Life Insurance Company Tower. Earnest Flagg's set back design concept would later cause problems for the Singer Tower which ultimately lead to its demise. The towers design did allow for less restrictive vertical space and increased sunlight on the smaller structures and in the streets below. It also restricted the amount of office space available per floor. The total area per floor was approximately 4,200 square feet. By 1960 the Singer Company lost control of their monopoly in the manufacturing of sewing machines due to increased competition and the influx of machines manufactured in Asian markets. These factors prompted the company to sell Bourne's monument later that year.

In 1963 a landmark preservationist named Alan Burnham classed the Singer building along with the Woolworth, Metropolitan Life and other buildings as important landmarks worthy of consideration of landmark status. In 1964 United States Steel bought the Singer Building. Unfortunately, the request by the landmarks preservation commission to save the Singer Building was weak. US Steel lobbied strong for the construction of a new building on the Singer sight. In August of 1967 demolition of the Singer Tower and its adjoining structures including the Bourne additions commenced. As the World Trade Center was being constructed in the Western portion of the city, the Singer Tower was being demolished. It would hold the record for being the tallest building to be demolished until September 11, 2001 with the attack on the World Trade Center.

Horses, Barns and Carriages

IN 1889 FREDERICK BOURNE PURCHASED four hundred acres of property on the Great South Bay of Long Island in the town of Oakdale, New York. Bourne would be the third purchaser of this piece of land. The first owner, William Nicoll purchased the Oakdale property along with thousands of additional acres surrounding it. The vast Nicoll Patent as it came to be known consisted of over fifty thousand acres. Part of it was purchased from the Secatogue Indians in the late 1600's. The property's ownership remained in the Nicoll family for nearly two hundred years until Louisa Nicoll, a descendant of the original owner married William Ludlow in 1841. She was given part of the Nicoll patent as part of her dowry, which included the land in Oakdale which later would be purchased by Mr. Bourne for $80,000.00. Most historians agree that it was the Ludlow's who gave the town of Oakdale its name. In 1890 Mr. Bourne would begin construction on the Oakdale estate.

On March 31, 1891 Frederick Bourne purchased the Lena Course Evans property located on the country road of Main Street in West Sayville. The purchase price was $14,500.00. It was an ancient structure with a history that dated back to pre-revolutionary times. The house was full of legend and had a rich history. In its earliest days, it was known as the Widow Molly Inn. The land on which it stood was part of the Nicoll Patent, a grant from the Crown before the revolution. Many of the older residents of the day spoke of legends of the home being haunted by ghosts and of dead sea pirates who at one time plundered it.

*Bourne purchased from Lena Course Evans the "Widow Molly House" in late March
1891. It was located on South Country Road in West Sayville between Rollstone and
Tyler Avenues. In 1913 the house was sectioned, the larger portion of which was moved to
West Street, now known as Dale Drive. In that same year it became the site of Marjorie
and Howard Bourne's Christmas party for children of Oakdale and West Sayville.*

Later in its history the home would become part of a darker legacy, having been inhabited by Lena Evans sister, Edith Course Evans. In 1912, Edith
would heroically lay down her life aboard the Titanic, giving up her seat
aboard one of the lifeboats to a mother and her two children. Edith would
later perish aboard the ill-fated steamer. The house with all its legacy and
charm was purchased as a temporary staging area for the Bourne family to
live in while their stables were being built a mile and a half west in Oakdale.
Lena Evans was a widow. Her grandfather was Israel Course; his occupation
was a tanner. The Course house had a large barn and a paddock area suited
for Mr. Bourne's fledgling collection of horses.

Despite the many improvements made to the stable, it was still inadequate for his needs. The first structures to be completed on the site of the Oakdale mansion were the horse stables. On July 24, 1893, a suspicious fire had destroyed the stables on the West Sayville site. During these early years' security was an issue. The Bourne's were newcomers to the area. Construction on the mansion in Oakdale increased employment and brought wealth to the local businesses. However, there were others who saw Bourne's acquisition of bay front property as a threat. Suspicions were at their highest in the summer and fall of 1893, a year which saw the burning of the West Sayville house. Most of the home was badly damaged by the blaze. The eastern most portion of the home was largely left intact with only smoke damage. The same year saw a portion of the barn and stables destroyed by fire and the suspicious death of Mr. Bourne's prize Hackney stallion Glendale.

Mr. Bourne quickly hired local carpenters and laborers to work on the reconstruction of the old Course house and on the barn and stable located on the property. By May 1894 the Bourne family could move back into the house. Mr. Bourne and his family did all they could to gentrify themselves with the locals and to curry their admiration and respect. In the summer of 1894 Arthur Bourne signed up to play third base for the local baseball team. The baseball field was located across the country road from their home in West Sayville on the south side. By May of 1895 Arthur would become captain of the team. His tenure on the team would become short lived, for in July he would injure himself in a collision with a bicycle.

The barn at West Sayville was rebuilt, but the site still had its problems. An infestation of rodents was an ongoing nuisance. Alexander Mair and his staff did all they could to curtail the infestation. The rat problem was the cause of a publicized event that occurred on June 5, 1896 when Alfred Bourne felt compelled to rid the barn of the rat problem single handedly by shooting them with his 22-caliber pistol. The Colt double action open top 22 caliber revolver had no trigger guard. While loading the little pistol the young man accidentally shot himself in the foot. The injury was not serious and Dr. Robinson was called to treat the wound. The house in West Sayville was meant to be a summer home for the Bourne's, however, during the summer of 1896 it appeared to take on the characteristics of a sanitarium for the sick and wounded.

In June baby Kenneth had his first mysterious attack which proved nearly fatal. In July Mr. Bourne, who was rapidly gaining the appeal and admiration of the locals put on what was to become an annual tradition of giving a firework display on the shores of the Great South Bay in West Sayville. Always desiring to be part of the action, Mr. Bourne sustained a severe burn to his hand while igniting a rocket. September saw two more incidents. On September 4th Alfred was on the rehabilitation list after also being hit by a bicycle in front of his house. Donations were requested for the construction of a bicycle path on Tyler Avenue, which was a street on the east corner of the Bourne property. Having had his sons sustain injuries from two bicycle accidents near his home, Mr. Bourne respectfully declined to contribute. On September 11, 1896 Marion, who was battling tonsillitis throughout the summer, had another flair up of the condition, this time causing a high fever. Dr. Robinson was again called to the house for treatment. She was sent to Manhattan and her tonsils were eventually removed.

Frederick Bourne and His Horses

By the middle of the decade of the 1880's Frederick Bourne had ascended into an executive position within the Singer Company. His rise into the world of aristocracy was now firmly in place. One of Mr. Bourne's earliest passions was to travel in grand style in elaborate carriages pulled by well bred horses. For the aristocrat, there was no grander entrance to an affair or function than to arrive by coach pulled by an elegant team of high stepping thoroughbreds. A breed of horse that was rapidly making its name as the finest bred driving horse of its day was the Hackney.

The Hackney's arrival into mainstream American horsemanship was relatively new at this time. Anglo maniac horse breeders of the day were critical of the Hackney breed. The origins of the breed began in Norfolk England. They came from the line of Norfolk trotters, selectively bred for elegance and speed. This was the golden age of driving, when automobiles were not even a dream. The first Hackney imported to America was 239 Stella, brought to Philadelphia by a Mr. A.J. Cassatt in 1878. Other Hackney enthusiasts along with Mr. Cassatt founded The American Hackney Horse Society in 1881.

The Hackney in appearance had several distinctive characteristics in which even a novice to horsemanship could easily discern amongst other horse breeds. First, its high arching neck and long body, causing a wide distance between its forelegs and hind legs when standing stretched out at full length. The Hackney has an "Aire" about him that is unmistakable. The second and most notable characteristic of this remarkable animal is its gate and movement. At first glance a well-trained Hackney is the showiest horse in existence. A good one when shown will electrify the crowd under the hands of a first-class handler or driver. The gate is an exaggerated high step with the front knee bending high and close to the chest. The hind legs come well forward with a powerful sweep, throwing the body upward and holding it poised while in forward movement. This gate is by no means instinctive to the breed, however, its overall confirmation allows for good development of its action.

To further develop the gate of a Hackney horse requires the skill of expert trainers. Frederick Bourne had in his charge some of the finest horse trainers of the day, the best of whom was Alexander Mair. Born in Scotland, Mr. Mair immigrated to the United States as a young man bringing with him an extensive knowledge of horsemanship which eventually enabled him to be employed by Mr. Bourne. In time, proving his ability, he would take charge of the breeding stables on the Indian Neck Farm. Another of Mr. Bourne's trainers was Jack McCreish, another Scotsman. Together along with other trainers the men developed a training style of lunging the horses through high stacks of loose hay which fostered the exaggerated gate that was a trademark of the Hackney breed.

Mr. Bourne spared no expense in acquiring the finest Hackney's that were available. By the spring of 1892 the stables at Indian Neck Farms were completed and soon well stocked. Among the most prominent at the stables were:

Evelena – A two-year-old Hackney mare.
Bay Maggie – A colt by Forest Prince.
Diana – One of the stables favorites, a three-year-old mare.
Czarevna – Three-year-old brown Hackney whose Dam was Brown Fashion and sired by Dagmar.
Shy Girl – An imported Hackney mare sired by Confidence. A Chicago breeder claimed of Confidence she showed the finer points of any animal of the Hackney class.
Dolce – A Hackney mare imported from England where she won five first prizes.

In addition to these well-bred Hackney's the stable also included at this time Ginger – A beautiful sorrel colored Kansas pony. A good jumper with plenty of speed and endurance. She had an even disposition and intelligent eye. Ginger responded well to commands and verbal prompts. Ginger was a favorite of young Arthur who was skilled at jumping her over 3 foot hurdles.

Dutchess – A Canadian hunter with a jumping record of over 6 feet.

Hispinola – A sorrel thoroughbred saddle horse used by all for pleasure riding.

Mr. Bourne on one of his prize saddle horses. Photo
courtesy of Robert and Patty Mondore.

Glendale

AMONG THE FINEST OF HORSES Mr. Bourne owned was a Hackney named Glendale. In the Spring of 1890 Frederick Bourne purchased Glendale from Mr. Garrett Taylor, the owner of Townhouse Breeders of Norwich, England. The purchase price was $25,000.00. This majestic stallion was foaled in 1887 and was entitled "the lord of the harem." He stood 15.2 hands. He was a handsome dark brown horse, with a spot on his face and white hind pasterns. He was perfect in style and action with remarkable speed. In England, he received four first prizes and four second prizes. His Dam was Kathleen and his sire was Confidence, the best Hackney blood in England. Their pedigrees had been traced back nearly two hundred years. Glendale's sire Confidence showed more prize winnings than any other stallion.

For all of Glendale's triumphs he would be best remembered by his mysterious and tragic death. The incident occurred sometime during the late evening or early morning hours of October 18, 1893. That evening Mr. Bourne was in Manhattan attending a late dinner party in honor of Lord Dunraven at the Knickerbocker Club. Earlier that evening at 9:00 pm Alexander Mair made his rounds in the stable before heading to bed. At that time, Glendale was standing, and looked well. Mr. Mair claimed that usually three men would sleep within the stable during the night and a watchman was supposed to be posted outside to watch over things around the estate and near the stable. Earlier that year on July 24th, the barn located at West Sayville had burned down. The horses and carriages were saved and no cause of the fire could be determined. Then on August 12th much of the old house on that location was destroyed. Despite the extra protection and the heightened awareness of suspicion, Glendale was found the next morning lying down in his stall, his four legs doubled-up and his rear legs stretched out.

Mr. Mair sent a rider to summon Dr. W. S. Gilbert, a veterinarian surgeon who lived in Bayport, New York. Upon arrival Dr. Gilbert examined Glendale along with Mr. Mair. An external examination showed no evidence of foul play. While examining the eyes, it was thought a blood vessel had ruptured but even that was inconclusive. Finally, an autopsy was performed which consisted of an examination of the stomach contents. There was no evidence of the consumption of any poison or any apparent toxins which would indicate the cause of death.

These were medically primitive times and of course no blood work was done from which today would give a clearer indication to the cause of death. There is no doubt that the incident was a great embarrassment for Mr. Mair. The newspapers wrote several articles speculating weather Mr. Bourne had enemies. The oystermen in particular were unhappy with the arrival of Mr. Bourne. Beginning in 1890 the owners of an oyster house located on a parcel of land purchased by Mr. Bourne were asked to vacate the property. This action caused great concern and was an inconvenience to the oystermen. The charge for carting oysters to a new location away from the beds would be over $2,000.00 a year.

The suspicious fires of 1893 along with the death of Glendale were a wakeup call for Mr. Mair and for Mr. Bourne both of whom would do everything they could to prove themselves as good neighbors. Mr. Mair from this time forward would hold greater accountability for his staff at the stables.

STARLIGHT—FIRST-PRIZE HACKNEY STALLION. The property of Mr. F. G. Bourne, of New York City.

There are no known photographs of Glendale, however he did sire the magnificent stallion Starlight, pictured above.

Enthorpe Performer

FREDERICK BOURNE WAS NOT UNDAUNTED by the death of Glendale. In 1893 Mr. Bourne purchased a 3-year-old prize winning Hackney named Enthorpe Performer from the stud farm of H. L. Higginson of Boston. The purchase price was $25,000.00 the same value of Glendale, however, with even greater talent and breeding. Enthorpe is registered in the American Hackney stud book as number 118.

He was of the Yorkshire breed and was bright bay colored with four white feet and a snip on his nose. Like Glendale, Enthorpe Performer was of the highest breeding, having been sired by the legendary Matchless of Londesburo. He resembled his sire and had the much coveted four white feet of his grand-sire Danegelt. His dam was Peg, by Superior; another champion of her lifetime.

Enthorpe Performer's high stepping gate was hailed by all who saw him as a sight to behold. He was 15 ¼ hands at height. He had a strong neck and a short back which allowed for what appeared to be an effortless action. Show goers were amazed at how much ground he could cover while exhibiting his beautiful strides. Enthorpe was a breathtaking animal and a true star taking blue ribbons in the New York Horse Show in 1894. He also took numerous first and second prizes in the preceding shows through the year 1899.

Enthorpe also performed magnificently as a stud. He sired numerous champions including Indian Prince and his bay mare sister Indian Queen both foaled at Indian Neck and winners of numerous ribbons at the Bay Shore Horse Show. The most outstanding of his foals was the bay mare

Princess Olga, whose dam was Czarevina. She took first prize for best 3-year-old Hackney mare in Philadelphia as well as first prize in harness. In addition, she won the American medal for best harness Hackney in that same show. In the New York Horse Show of 1899 Princess Olga took first place in harness pairs along with His Grace, in addition to three other first and second ribbons. Mr. Bourne's greatest success in horse showing occurred at the New York Horse Show in 1899 with his winning of the breeder's challenge cup. The award went to Mr. Bourne's Hackney Mare the Squaw. In addition to the cup there was also a $500.00 cash prize with the reserve ribbon going to Princess Olga. Enthorpe Performer had proved his worth in every way and is known in history as one of the greatest Hackney horses of all time.

Another star of the Indian Neck stables was the Russian Orloff "high school" (Haute Ecole) saddle stallion: Ad. The Orloff mounts were among the first breed of horses developed in Russia for use in their cavalry. This breed dates to the 18th century in an era when Russia was at war with Turkey. The horse derived its name from the Orloff brothers who were the favorite horse breeders of Catherine II of Russia. The Orloff brothers used Arabia, Thorobred, and Karabakh Turkish and Danish horse stock. They carefully handpicked their foundation stock to perfect this noble breed. Orloff's were elegant and strikingly beautiful, usually black in color with large expressive eyes, a swanlike neck, and superb topline. The confirmation of their legs were strong, straight and clean.

Like all Orlov's, Ad was a tall horse for his time at 15.3 hands. He was foaled in 1885 and for the next fifteen years he would be among the top ribbon winners in the high school / dressage events. Unlike many dressage horses Ad's tail was never docked. It was long and flowing with a long and beautiful wave which helped to accentuate his movements. He could walk "Spanish" and could go through all the movements riders demanded of a fine dressage horse while making it look nearly effortless. The Orloff breed was used extensively by the Russian cavalry during the first World War. Its high casualty rate nearly wiped the breed out of its existence. The coming of the Soviet regime and the popularization of the automobile further drove the breed to near extinction, however, a few breeders remained and today the Orlov's are making a resurgence.

By the closing decade of the 19th century horses had established themselves as the traditional and familiar source of power needed to move America through its journey in the industrial revolution. In a more abstract sense, by their very size, strength and beauty, horses symbolize a sublime representation of the power of humanity. This was especially true for aristocratic society. A well-bred horse through pedigree and breeding was a symbol for nobility and high society. Frederick Bourne's motivations for acquiring a stable of horses was not only fostered for practical purposes. Mr. Bourne also had a great love for all animals and a particular fondness for horses. This was a well-known fact in his day and by 1902 he was unanimously elected as a board member to the SPCA. He demanded that his horses be treated with the greatest respect and that their training and workload never be too harsh or demanding.

ENTHORPE PERFORMER—CHAMPION HACKNEY. Owned and exhibited by Mr. F. G. Bourne, of New York City.

The New York Horse Show

THE NEW YORK HORSE SHOW was another venue in horsemanship that Mr. Bourne particularly enjoyed. The show was societies premier event heralding the beginning of the New York fashionable fall season. It was the extravaganza of its day. It was not merely for the showing of horses and acquisition of ribbons and prize money. The New York Horse Show was a social gathering of societies elite. It was also a rare opportunity for ordinary people to witness aristocratic society in all its glory.

The New York Horse Show was held at the old Madison Square Garden. It was an assemblage of the smart, smarter and smartest sets, as well as fashion critics, celebrities, dress makers, the Nuevo rich and trade people along with the curious members of the middle class who for the price of an entry ticket could witness this aristocratic parade.

From a social point of view, the horse show was a scene of many triumphs for some of the more well-known families of the day. The Bourne's were not excluded. For the socially ambitious, a box at the horse show represented the beginning of a career in New York society. It was a place to catch the attention of the media and to have your name mentioned in both word and print with those of the leading celebrities of the day, notably the Astor's, The Vanderbilt's and The Roosevelt's. At a time before movie stars, aristocrats were among the most sought after celebrities of their time.

Mr. Bourne took no exception to the manner of dress for the participation and attendance of this rather formal affair. Morning and early afternoons were spent attending to the needs and preparation of the horses. At this time, it was typical to be dressed casually. By two o'clock in the afternoon it was required that a gentleman wore the regulation dress, typically a frock coat and or a waist coat of the same material usually worsted wool, double or single breasted. Trousers were typically stripped worsted wool in dark tones. A high silk hat, white shirt with attached cuffs and a lap wing collar. Additionally, light toned ascot gray suede gloves, patent leather or varnished calf skin boots with button tops were also worn. Mr. Bourne was one of the most handsomely dressed men of his day!

Newspaper columns covering the New York Horse Show were usually divided, one devoted to the horses and the rest on the women in attendance and their gossip. This horse show was the instrument on which fashionable society played. However, to the more serious horse breeders like Mr. Bourne the emphasis was on the horses. For the first several years of his participation in the New York Horse Show starting in the late 1880's, Mr. Bourne enjoyed the pomp and circumstance that surrounded it. By the close of the century he had grown weary of the circus like atmosphere of the show. Mr. Bourne was also disenchanted with the logistical problem associated with transporting the horses, especially with the shows located in Philadelphia and New England. The horses had to be transported by rail which was an extremely time consuming and labor intensive process. During this process, it was not unusual for the horses to sustain minor injuries to their feet or legs which for a show horse could greatly diminish their chances for success. This fact was also troubling for Mr. Bourne because he did not want his horses injured. Although he spared no expense at making the journey as comfortable as possible, he knew that a long ride in a rail car was distressing for the horses. Surely there could be a way to hold a horse show closer to home in a style to that of the New York Horse Show and away from all the madness of the large city.

The Bay Shore Horse Show

THE ANSWER TO MR. BOURNE'S New York Horse Show dilemmas would be the institution of the Bay Shore Horse Show. By the beginning of the 20th century what is now known as the Gold Coast of Long Island was firmly in place. On the great estates of Long Island, it was not uncommon to find a stable filled with horses for both showing and racing. Other wealthy horse owners in the area shared Mr. Bourne's concerns about the transportation issues and the snobbish, circus like atmosphere associated with the New York Horse Show. For these reasons the Bay Shore Horse Show was formed.

The first Bay Shore Horse Show was held on August 8th and 9th in 1901. The location of the show was held on the grounds of the old Oakwood Park which was at the extreme end of the town of Bay Shore about a mile north of the bay. Unlike the New York Horse Show the Bay Shore Horse Show was an open-air event. Sponsors of the show poured thousands of dollars into the development of the site to insure it would have a look of legitimacy and respectability. There was a deliberate attempt to shy away from the use of tents to not facilitate the look of a carnival like atmosphere. The site was leased from the town, and with the towns blessing a fine grand stand was erected for viewing. There were also commodious stables at the grand stands side and a first-rate paddock out front. Surrounding the paddock was a half mile track which was used for driving events. The list of investors in the show contained over 50 names the most prominent of whom was Frederick Bourne.

The new century brought with it a new list of stars coming out of the Indian Neck Stables. Enthorpe Performer proved his greatness not only in the show ring but also as a stud. His list of champion sires included Indian Prince and Indian Queen. This next generation also succeeded in the show ring and garnered numerous cash prizes and ribbons. During the first three years of the show the most coveted prizes were the silver cups for best in show. The cups were presented by the horse show association and another was presented and sponsored by the Brooklyn Eagle Daily Newspaper. By 1904 another cup was added to the list of prizes to be presented. This was "THE BOURNE CUP". In addition to the cup came a $250.00 cash prize which was donated to the event by Mr. Bourne himself. The Bourne Cup was the most prestigious prize awarded during this time. The trophy was for gig horse competition. A gig is a light, two wheeled cart capable of carrying one or two passengers and is pulled by one horse. The rules for winning the Bourne Cup called for the same owner of the same horse competing to win first prize two years in a row.

Every effort was made to make the Bay Shore Horse Show as prestigious as the New York Horse Show. The first years of the show were very successful and it was covered by the press extensively. It also had a significant following with New York society. However, despite all their efforts the Bay Shore Horse Show did not receive the national attention and participation that the New York Horse Show enjoyed. By 1910 the Bay Shore Horse Show had lost its footing in the main stream horse community. Frederick Bourne's interest had also waned. After the fire that destroyed his stables in 1909, Mr. Bourne sold off much of his show stock. With the coming of the age of the automobile his passions had switched to all things motorized.

Bourne Builds His Estate

MR. BOURNE FOUND THE IDEAL spot for which he had long been searching. The lands proximity to the Great South Bay was ideal for his yachting interests. Additionally, the area had become popular among the wealthy. The South Side Sportsman's Club was nearby. Popular for its abundance of trout fishing and duck hunting. Also, neighboring the Bourne estate was the eight-hundred-acre estate owned by W.K. Vanderbilt and Westbrook Farm, the two-thousand-acre estate of W. Bayard Cutting. The location was ideal, however, there was much work to be done. Much of the land was over grown with briers and brambles. There were swamps, thickets and miry places; thickly wooded areas which required clearing. He hired an army of local workers, employing scores of men to till and clear the land into fertile fields. He hired F.D. Brown to oversee the undertaking. Under Brown's leadership the fields were tilled and cleared. The paddock for the horses were seeded and soon a luxurious growth of grass was formed. Swamps were drained and trees thinned. Environing a portion of the land, a wide canal had been dug from which the high fresh water table of this land sprung from the earth. Also installed was a largemouth bass hatchery which provided the newly formed fresh water lakes with a well-stocked population of fish, the descendants of which the author would as a boy spend many a lazy summer afternoon fishing with his friends.

With the property beautified and revitalized it was christened "Indian Neck Farm." The name was derived from the fact that Indians had once lived on this land pre-dating the arrival of William Nicoll to the new world from England in 1664. Indian Neck would remain solely as the site of Mr. Bourne's horse farm for the better part of the 1890's. Bourne had obligations to the Singer Company and with Alfred Clark. Both of whom required his presence in New York City for extended periods of time. His vision of what he wanted his mansion to be was grand. It would require a small fortune to build and furnish the structure to fit his vision. After Alfred Clark's death in 1896 Bourne would acquire additional stock holdings in Singer that would allow the funding for his new home. More importantly, Clarke's death also freed Bourne from many of the obligations put on him by Clark regarding the time Bourne was required to give to the Singer Company. Alfred Corning Clark also willed to his Godson Alfred Severin Bourne the sum of $1M dollars. The newly acquired additional wealth and time enabled Bourne to finally realize the construction of his home in Oakdale.

Once again Bourne called upon his favorite architect Earnest Flagg to design the mansion. The Maryland and Virginia colonial designed home would have unobstructed views of the Great South Bay. By June of 1897 the foundation for the mansion was completed. On the foundation, would stand Flagg's design for the mansion. Built of brick and white marble trimmings, the home would occupy an area of three hundred feet long by one hundred twenty- five feet deep with a total of one hundred rooms. The work by the masons proceeded at a rapid pace. On October 29, 1897, the roof was completed. On November 5th Mr. Bourne threw a small party for his workers to celebrate the roofs completion.

The carpenters worked throughout the winter and spring of that year. There was much cause for celebration that summer, however, it was not without problems. In July Alexander Mair became ill with fever and was laid up for several weeks, perhaps an early flare up of his appendix. The new facility and its equine inhabitants would not be neglected despite Mr. Mair's absence. In that year, additional laborer quarters were completed thus increasing the number of workers at the mansion.

With the expanded laborer quarters came an increase in the number of employees hired to care for the horses. They were among the best that could be found and included brothers Robert, James and Joseph McCook of Canada, Stableman Frank Carshick, the Virginian James Bledso, private express man for the mail, William McCutcheon, private blacksmith and farrier, and Frank Rance, Coachman. In charge of it all was Superintendent Donald McKenzie who along with his wife lived in a large newly built cottage on the property.

The new stables would be the most state of the art design for its day and included wide aisles and runways, box stalls with cross ventilation, modern drains, wash rooms and feed boxes. A large harness room with ample cabinets and a rub down room was also included West of the barn near the bay was a half mile track where the horses could be exercised.

By the fall of 1897 Alexander Mair had recuperated from his illness and was in fine form for the New York Horse Show that year. Their best showing was that of Glendale's bay stallion Starlight, who took first prize in his class for stallions 3 years old and over. Enthorpe Performer took home third prize that year. His poor showing was extremely controversial. Indian Neck stables would continue to be one of the most successfully run stables in New York State. Every known modern improvement that was available was incorporated into its planning and construction. In addition, the latest styles of carriages, runabouts and other wagons were purchased and enjoyed. Here also were the highest bred Jersey cows, dogs, chickens and exotic foul.

On December 28, 1900 Donald McKenzie died of heart disease. With McKenzie's passing Alexander Mair took over as Superintendent of the Bourne estate as well as the management of Indian Neck farms and stables. The first decade of the 20th century at Indian Neck would be a time of both triumph and tragedy. Both Mr. Bourne and Alexander Mair had high ambitions on making Indian Neck a profitable and successful venture. In the summer of 1902 they experimented with the planting of 15 acres of kale seed. The venture proved successful. The 15 acres planted yielded about 2,000 pounds of seed per acre which resulted a sizable profit. Mr. Bourne's farm employed a great number of inhabitants in the area bringing wealth and prosperity to the community and its businesses.

As with every farm and with every success comes its share of hardship. In October 1902, an epidemic of hog cholera swept through the farm and killed almost the entire stock of pigs. At or around the same time several of the horses were lost due to sever cases of colic. By the winter of 1902 things began to look better. Frederick Bourne was elected Vice Commodore of the New York Yacht Club that December. He also celebrated a belated 50th birthday that month with a lavish party in his honor at the estate.

The interior of the home would require a great deal more time to complete. On June 3, 1898, the carpentry contractors of Sloan and Maller were hired to begin its construction. Earlier in that same year on February 4th Albert Sweeney was hired to build the homes' staircases. A description of the mansions interior was best described in a May 24, 1902 edition of Town and Country: *"Entering the house you are greeted by a great hall twenty-four feet wide and thirty feet long. A large fire place, with the hearth and facings of Sienna marble, suggest a favorite lounging place in the chill of Autumn nights. The floors throughout the house are of oak in parquet style, softened in many places by rugs and skins. The stairway leading from the hall forms at the turn a broad, semicircular landing, fitted with cozy seats and corners. On the right of the entrance is the drawing room, finished in cherry, covered with white enamel. The wall panels are of rich brocaded patterns. From the ceiling is suspended a massive chandelier.*

Beyond the drawing room is the library. A room in which Mr. Bourne has taken the greatest pride and interest inspired by his long associations with the Mercantile Library some years ago. His great collections of valuable editions and rare prints are arranged in small bookcases about the room. Broad comfortable couches and chairs invite easy indolence here. The music and morning rooms adjoin the drawing-room and library. The former contains a fine organ the pipes of which extend through two stories. A piano and harp provide means of other forms of music. In the rear of this part of the house is a large semi-circular balcony, from which rise colonial columns almost the height of the house. A veranda borders the morning room and music rooms and leads to another one, much larger and rectangular in shape opening from the billiard room. This wing also contains on the lower floor complete Turkish bath equipment, including a large swimming pool.

On the left of the entrance hall are the dining and breakfast rooms and the conservatory beyond. The last is eighty feet long and half as broad, and is two stories high. The front part of the wing is used for the kitchen culinary quarters and servant's rooms. To provide liberal accommodations for the entertainments of his friends, Mr. Bourne had the two principal groups of rooms arranged ensuite, so that they could be thrown together when the occasion required." Flagg's design called for the sleeping quarters to be on the second floor.

While work was proceeding on the interior of the house the landscaping and infrastructure on the grounds were also moving along at a steady pace. Additional landscape architects who had recently completed the grounds surrounding the Chicago Exposition were hired to further enhance the landscape designs. Over ten thousand trees and shrubs were planted. A fine driveway leading from the main road up to the house was construct-ed. Magnificent iron gates were installed along the front perimeter of the main road. A gate lodge was built at the entrance as a shelter for security personnel.

A colonnade of pillars marked the intersections along the roads on the estate. Later, the same style pillars were constructed along the entranceway to Oakdale's first neighborhood on what was known as Chicken Street. Mr. Bourne owned several lots and houses on Chicken Street. Bourne provided these homes for many of the families who worked on his estate. He was not fond of the name "Chicken Street" and petitioned the highway commission-ers of the Town of Islip to change its name. On July 26, 1895, they formally accepted the name change of the thoroughfare. The name was changed to West Street, for at that time the street was situated a mile west of the Bourne's temporary home in West Sayville.

The monumental task of completing the Bourne mansion was achieved by the closing weeks of the 19th century. The dawn of the new century and the official opening of their new home was a cause for celebration. Coincidentally, it was also Mr. and Mrs. Bourne's 25th wedding anniversary. On February 9, 1900, the day of their anniversary, they threw open the doors of their new home and hosted a party the likes of which had never been seen in the area. Several hundred guests were invited. Special parlor cars belonging to the Long Island Rail Road were reserved by Mr. Bourne. At Long Island City, the cars awaited guests arriving from Manhattan. From there they would be transported to the station at Oakdale in style and comfort. The reception was from 4:00 to 7:00 and was followed by dancing.

Mr. and Mrs. Bourne received their guests in the main hall where for days, workers were busy transforming the area with floral decorations consisting of white roses and ropes of laurels covered with silver spangles. A profusion of palms and banks of lilies, ferns and azaleas were generously situated throughout the homes interior all of which were imported from greenhouses from wherever available.

The grounds were illuminated with over fifteen hundred electric lights which at the time made for a magnificent spectacle. The music for the reception was furnished by The Landor's Orchestra. Mr. and Mrs. Bourne's young daughters wore white and gray domino dresses covered with silver stars and spangles. Older guests stayed and mingled for a while after a delightful dinner which was served in the large dining hall. Mr. Bourne's senior guests were delighted and upon departure were again transported back to Manhattan in the same style from which they arrived. The younger guests danced well into the evening, many of whom remained overnight. In true Victorian fashion, the entire upper story had been arranged for the comfort of the young ladies, while the basement had been especially fitted for the entertainment of the young men.

With the celebration over and the Bourne home transferred back to its original state, the family went on to live in the house for many years to come. There would be many other events and celebrations. Mr. Bourne would continue to add to the magnificence and charm to the estate for the remainder of his life. The Bourne's were the proprietors of several other residences, but Indian Neck would always be the place the entire family called home.

FIG. 68. DRAWING ROOM, RESIDENCE OF F. G. BOURNE, ESQ., OAKDALE, L. I.
The woodwork is of cherry, covered with white enamel; the floor is of oak, and the panels are covered with a rich brocade.

The Bourne's Oakdale Mansion (Indian Neck) was featured in the "May 24, 1902 Edition" of the Town and Country Magazine: This photo of the Mansion's drawing room depicts two of the many animal skin rugs that were among Mr. Bourne's "Trophies." Like Theodore Roosevelt Mr. Bourne was a concerned conversationalist and was involved in the preservation of land for wildlife. A paradox not easily understood in today's world.

FIG. 70. MUSIC ROOM IN RESIDENCE OF F. G. BOURNE, ESQ., OAKDALE, L. I.

The Great Race of 1908

ALEXANDER MAIR'S STEWARDSHIP AS SUPERINTENDENT was proving successful and for the most part there was happiness amongst the workers on the estate. It was an eclectic group of men and women who labored there. Irishmen, English, Scotts, Italian laborers, Canadian Stableman, and Dutch and Bohemian farm workers, French house servants and maids all working together and for the most part getting along. Without exception, it would be nearly impossible to have such an eclectic group of people working together without there being an occasional conflict, confrontation or competition.

The IV Olympic games of 1908 were ending on October 30th. Newspapers gave extensive coverage on the games which occurred in London that year. The games were much better organized than previous games. They were the first Olympic games to include an opening ceremony. The games were originally scheduled to be played in Rome, however, the eruption of Mount Vesuvius in 1906 forced their relocation. The games were marred by politics and nationalism. Great Britain's continued refusal to give Ireland its independence caused the games to be boycotted by the Irish athletes, in addition, American athletes agreed not to dip the American flag to the British Royals during the opening ceremonies.

There was also controversy over the final 400-meter heat. In the race, United States Runners W.C. Robins and J.C. Carpenter were running first and second respectively around the last turn of the track. Third place runner Wyndham Halswelle of Britain attempted to pass the Americans when someone shouted "foul!" Carpenter broke the tape in first with Robins finishing second and Halswelle third. British officials accuse Carpenter of blocking and elbowing Halswelle and voided the race, ordering it to be rerun. The American's refused and protested the ruling which resulted in Halswelle running the race by himself.

There was much banter over the controversy back at Indian Neck stables, especially between the English and American stable workers. For the last 50 years-well before the first Olympic games in 1896, runners from Great Britain completely dominated the records for the mile run as well as other events. The first and second finish by the Americans was a humiliation to British pride. It was well known at Indian Neck that there were two of the fastest runners working at the stables. Jack McDearmid, also of British decent, was proud of his heritage. He had run several races against other stable workers and had never been beaten. Edward Thorp, an American, was a newcomer to Indian Neck. The 20-year-old was a superb athlete working as a groom and hot walker for the horses. After much boasting between the two young men and much arguing over the outcome of the 400-meter final it was decided that the two men would have a foot race twice around the half mile track to settle the score. Word of the competition spread throughout the estate and there was considerable betting on its outcome. Before long the news spread throughout town and by the next morning a large crowd gathered around the track to watch the outcome of the event. For the winner, there was a $5.00 prize provided by the Bourne family.

At the starting line the men shook hands and a pistol was fired to start the race. Thorp kept a good pace alongside the Englishman. But the determined McDearmid's speed was too much for the young American. At the finish line McDearmid won over the American competitor by three yards with an astonishing reported time of four minutes twenty-seven seconds. For the moment, the British had prevailed, but it was a new century and an American century. It would take another 4 years and another Thorpe – Jim Thorpe to usher in Americas dominance in track and field by winning the decathlon in the 1912 Olympics in Stockholm Sweden.

By the winter of 1909 other conflicts occurred. Alexander Mair held high standards for the staff at Indian Neck. Any worker failing to perform their duty to his standards would be reprimanded or fired. On February 10, 1909, there was an incident which led to the firing of Mr. Bourne's head coachmen Stephen Vile and two grooms, one of which was Jack McDearmid. Mr. Mair had discharged McDearmid for persistent absences and in being derelict in his duties at the farm. Stephen Vile hailed from Great Britain. During the discussion between Mair and McDearmid Vile had stepped in to the defense of his countryman. Despite their objections, Mair would have none of this, and discharged Stephen Vile and the two grooms.

News of the incident was sent to Mr. Bourne. He had recently departed to Brunswick Georgia on a six-week hunting excursion in the alligator bogs. He brought three of his best hunting horses with him but of course was concerned about the unrest back at Indian Neck. It was just the previous year on January 31, 1908 that night watchman McFadden had caught prowlers on the estate. Then again on February 1st another attempt to rob the estate was foiled by the watchman. This time he fired his pistol at the would-be burglars who made good their escape. During the summer of 1908 a story had broken about an alleged jewel theft at Indian Neck. This story, other rumors, and publicized articles about secret treasure chambers located on the estate may have be the impetus for the attempted heists. Mr. Bourne would increase the security presence located on the estate from then on.

The Bourne Family
and Their Dogs

COINCIDING WITH FREDERICK BOURNE'S INTEREST in horses was his great love of dogs. The kennels which housed Mr. Bourne's hunting dogs were built at the same time the stables were being constructed at Indian Neck. The Bourne's were also found of show dogs. One of the family's earliest stars in the show circuit was their prized St. Bernard Sultan III. Sultan was bred and raised by Edward Roche. Roche and his wife were well known dog breeders. He was the proprietor of the Tackapousha House Resort located in Far Rockaway. Mr. Bourne purchased Sultan sometime in 1890. In the Westminster Kennel show of 1891 Sultan III took a prize-winning ribbon for his breed.

Marion was the family member who held the greatest admiration for dogs. Marion had a particular fondness for Russian Wolfhounds, also known as Borzois which loosely translates in Russian as "fast dog". Similar in appearance to a Greyhound, they are a long haired quiet dog with gracious house manners. Not unlike her dogs, Marion enjoyed spending a large amount of time at home. In fact, in a letter dated November 8, 1912 Frederick Bourne writes to his daughter May *"Marion does not take quiet enough outdoor exercise and we are trying to get her out"*. When Marion was seen out on the estate it was quite often with the accompaniment of her Wolfhounds. She allowed them ample exercise on the spacious lawns. Marion's Wolfhounds were frequent winners at dog shows including the annual shows of the Westminster

Kennel Club. In the February 1907 show, her young Wolfhound named Michael Strogoff won first prize in the puppy's class. She also owned a magnificent pair of pure White Hounds which are believed to have been purchased for upwards of $3,000.00. At the Cedarhurst Kennel Club Show of 1905 Marion's Wolfhounds Czar of Tamboff captured a reserved ribbon. She was also awarded the prize for "the best dog owned by a woman".

At any given time on Indian Neck at least a half dozen or more dogs could be out working with the field hands or stable workers. The dogs were especially valuable around the stables where at night they would stand guard along with the night stable watchman. On the night of August 16, 1905, a shocking incident occurred in the horse stables, instilling terror in both the stable hands and the dogs. That evening there were severe thunderstorms. Angry clouds billowed a dark cast on the twilight lit sky. Streaks of sheet lightening flashed across the sky, the light from which created a mild chorus of intrepid baying from the stalls. The ozone laidened air became electrified, its odor overpowering all others. While the watch dogs laid quietly, a sudden brilliant illumination filled the isles. The phenomena known as ball lightening had entered the stable opening, startling the dogs who in an instant gave chase to the glowing spheres. In the next instant, a crash of thunder boomed. Both man and dog fled in panic. Later a search party was sent out for the dogs. They were not found until the evening of the next day. With some reassurance, they were prompted back to home none the worse for wear. One of the dogs nearly lost was one of Mr. Bourne's eight prized hunting dogs. This was not the first incident where Mr. Bourne's dogs were mishandled. By July of the following year, Mr. Bourne had a special kennel constructed in the center of the game preserve at Oakdale. It was located at a point midway between Indian Neck and the town of Bohemia. His object was to keep the eight hunting dogs separate from the some 30 or more dogs owned by Marion and others. In addition to the new kennels, pheasant pens were constructed in which a young stock of pheasants could be kept and bred for hunting purposes.

Hunting was a favorite leisure activity for Mr. Bourne. Later in history golf would take over as a sport for businessmen. During Mr. Bourne's time hunting was the preferred sport amongst gentlemen of business.

Marion Bourne and her champion Russian Wolfhound Michel Strogoff.

Bourne and the Fire Department

Despite the precautions taken, nothing could have prepared the residence of Indian Neck for the destructive fire that occurred on October 2, 1909. The fire had completely destroyed the carriage house and stables. It was an enormous blaze that lit the night sky and could be seen for miles. Alexander Mair had gathered the men together to form a corp to fight the blaze. Fire departments from Sayville and West Sayville were also summoned. There were problems. The hydrants on the Bourne estate were not compatible with the regulation hose on the pumping apparatus and no adaptor could be found. Additionally, the water pressure was inadequate causing the men to resort to a bucket brigade for much of the fight.

By the time things could be organized the fire took hold with an intense ferocity. Mair and his men had heroically managed to remove all the panicking horses from their stalls and bring them to the safety of the corral near the track. In addition, all the carriages were saved from destruction. With the stables fully involved, the fire fight was concentrated on exposure by protecting nearby structures from ignition. The force was marshalled by the automobile garage which was located some 20 yards away from the stables and filled with several costly automobiles and gasoline. Mr. Bourne had personally attended to help remove the automobiles to safety.

The blaze was discovered at 6:45pm. By 8:30pm reinforcements had arrived from Sayville. The fire was successfully contained until it burned itself out. Daylight revealed the stables in complete ruin. On the second floor of the structure were housed the stablemen and the grooms, all of whom had lost their personal possessions and sums of money. Mr. Bourne had reimbursed the men for their losses.

Mr. Bourne had good relations with the local fire departments since the time he first moved into the area. When the Bourne's moved to West Sayville the entire community was in the midst of a dynamic change in its history, one in which Mr. Bourne would have a profound effect. By 1891 even its name would undergo a change. On May 13th of that year a meeting was held at Dingman Van Popering's store. The sleepy little town then known as Greenville was unanimously christened by its new name of West Sayville. Even before the name of the village had been decided there was talk of organizing a hook and ladder company as early as 1890. On October 1, 1891, a meeting was once again held in Van Popering's store. The charter for the newly formed organization was received on January 23, 1892. In a role call given on May 6, 1892, thirty-two voices replied. On June 3, 1892, a committee was formed to start plans for the construction of a firehouse. The plans moved along swiftly and by June 15th work on the firehouse commenced. Otto Thames was the carpenter who was hired to build the new facility. The price of the contract was $700.00.

On May 28, 1892, the Bourne family was in residence at their West Sayville house. The newly formed fire department was in need of funding. Mr. Bourne purchased for the West Sayville Fire Department a bell on which the alarm for fires were rung for the next forty years until the construction of the new firehouse in 1931. In addition to the bell Bourne also purchased for the West Sayville Fire Department a hand drawn hook and ladder truck. Many years later the old timers who pulled the ladder truck remarked to the author that pulling the apparatus was a laborious task and when responding to an alarm at the Bourne estate: "They would get their second wind at Chicken Street." Bourne was also a member of the Sayville Fire Department to whom he also showed great generosity. In 1916 he donated to the Sayville Fire Departments Hook and Ladder Company No. 1 a combination motor driven chemical engine and hose wagon made by the REO Motor Car Company.

Bourne joined the fire department on the suggestion of architect I. H. Green. Bourne maintained cordial relations with the architect and called on him on numerous occasions to design the homes Bourne had built for his workers in the community. Green's architectural designs were an important part of the evolution of the community. His Dutch Colonial Revival motifs contrasted with the traditional designs of the day, that being Queen Anne, Craftsman and Bungalow styles. His Dutch Colonials featured gambrel roofs, flared eaves and generously sized porches with stout columns. The Sayville and West Sayville area were predominately populated by Dutch settlers. Green's designs were in concert with the traditions of these settlers, many of whom were members of the fire department and people with whom he and Mr. Bourne embraced with affection.

The horses, carriages and stable workers were relocated to Mr. Bourne's house in West Sayville until a new facility could be built. By March 1910 a final decision was made by Mr. Bourne to tear down all the existing cow stables, dairy buildings, poultry houses, machine shop and blacksmith facilities located on the Indian Neck estate. Plans for a new state of the art facility were prepared by Burnett and Hopkins of New York City. After the completion of the blueprints, construction was put into the very capable hands of William Bason and Sons, a well-known Long Island company.

The new farm building was constructed just a quarter mile north of the main estate on a large parcel of land purchased by Mr. Bourne some years earlier. It was located at the head of West Street Formerly Chicken Street and just south of the Long Island Railroad station adjacent to the tracks. The buildings were constructed of concrete with an exterior finish coat of white stucco. The animal stalls would be constructed of fire proof concrete, with concrete floors fitted with drains. There was an elaborate plumbing system which tied all the floor drains to hose connections so the stalls could be easily flushed out and cleaned. An improved state of the art ventilation system was also installed throughout the stables and barns.

The dairy house was fitted with a large steam boiler. It would provide an abundance of steam and hot water for sterilizing and cleaning. The memory of the hog cholera epidemic was still fresh in everyone's mind. The new facility would incorporate every modern form of cleaning and sterilization apparatus available to insure such an incident could never happen again. There would also be fire hydrants located on the farm with stand pipes and connections of the latest type. The horse stables contained twenty-eight stalls for the farm horses. Located near the horse stables was an immense hay barn. The most notable feature of the new facility was the 80-foot water tower and tank which was surmounted with a windmill. The windmill in Oakdale was to become one of the most enduring legacies of the Bourne estate.

On June 3, 1892 construction begins on West Sayville's first firehouse. That same year Bourne donated this bell and hand drawn hook and ladder truck to the newly formed Fire Department. Photo by Philip Selvaggio with permission and courtesy of West Sayville Fire Department.

In 1906 Bourne donated this REO Combination Chemical Engine and Hose Truck. It's four-cylinder engine was capable of developing a speed of 35 miles per hour. It housed two 35-gallon copper tanks for holding firefighting chemicals and a reel carrying 200 feet of four-ply chemical hose, a 24-foot ladder, a 10-inch locomotive bell and a hand siren. Photo courtesy of R. Byne.

Kenneth

THE BOURNE FAMILY WAS GROWING rapidly by the beginning of the 1890's. With the family firmly entrenched at their Dakota Apartment in New York City and Mr. Bourne equally entrenched with the business at Singer, there appeared to be little likelihood that a permanent move away from the city could happen anytime soon. At this time, Mr. Bourne's most passionate pastime was horses. There was a horse stable facility built across from the Dakota Apartment complex, but it was not adequate for Mr. Bourne's every expanding collection of horse flesh. In 1890, he began construction of his new state of the art facility located on his newly acquired land in Oakdale. At this time, Albert Clark was still alive. Mr. Bourne's commitment to the Singer Company and Mr. Clark were binding. It would be impossible to sustain this commitment away from Manhattan. What was needed was a larger country home close to the new stables in Oakdale. A place where his children could escape into a more rural setting and enjoy the outdoors.

By 1891 Mrs. Bourne was pregnant, further pressing the necessity for more room. By April 1891 just such a house came available in the hamlet of West Sayville. The house was once a large country inn which was now owned by Lena Course. The Course family had lived in the old home for a decade. The house was purchased by Lena's grandfather Israel Course in 1881 from a gentleman named Charles A. Frost. Mr. Course was the co-owner of a tanning facility named Course and Pratt located at 83 Gold

Street in an area of Manhattan that was known as "The Swamp". Mr. Course invested his time and money fixing up the old Frost place which would be a summer residence for his granddaughters Lena and Edith. On July 17, 1885 Israel Course died and six years later Lena sold the house to Mr. Bourne.

The legacy of the old Course place stretched back much further than its former resident Charles A. Frost. It was a residence that was filled with local stories and legends which dated back to pre-revolutionary times. The house was located next door to the old Green house on South Country Road now Montauk Highway. It is a historical fact that George Washington stopped at the Green home during a journey across Long Island in 1791. The Course home was then known as "The Widow Molly Inn". A legend surrounding the Widow Molly and the Inn is recounted in a book published in 1895 written by Edward Richard Shaw entitled Legends of Fire Island Beach and the South Side. In the book, Mr. Shaw tells a rather dramatic story of the Widow Molly, keeper of the Inn, a beloved suitor and its heroic effort in fighting off pirates. The pirates were hell bent on plundering the Inn of its silverware and trusted musket belonging to the hero in addition to doing harm to the Widow Molly and her servant.

The houses legend was well known to the locals long before the publishing of the book and added to the charm of the residence. By the spring of 1891 the Bourne family had moved into the Course residence and on May 26, 1891 their son Kenneth was born. The surviving children now numbering 8 were delighted with their new home. The older boys quickly gentrified themselves with the locals. Eighteen-year-old Arthur would play baseball for the Sayville team. The delight of the family was baby Kenneth who was described as a "particularly bright and winsome lad". With other preschoolers to attend to George, age 3, and Marjorie, age 1, Mrs. Bourne's 2 eldest daughters May age 10 and Marion age 9 would help mother tend to the newborn and grew found of their role as junior surrogate nannies. Indeed, by this time the Bourne's also had sufficient title for the employment of hired help including nannies and servants.

The following summer of 1892 the Bourne family returned to their summer home in West Sayville with Mr. Bourne making frequent trips from Manhattan to be with his family and to check the progress of the stables and the horses. When the West Sayville house caught fire the following year, Mr. Bourne quickly had the sections of the damaged house rebuilt and by May of 1894 the family could resume their habitation in the structure. The summer of 1895 and 1896 once again saw the family back in West Sayville. By this time the stables in Oakdale and the other structures needed for the stable workers and caretakers were also completed. Mr. Bourne had acquired his first substantial yacht, the Revere. A boathouse was also built for Mr. Bourne's growing interest in yachting. The family was now making frequent trips in their new sea vessels along the south shore of Long Island. The horses were winning ribbons at the New York Horse Show and life for the most part was good.

On June 26, 1896 3-year-old Kenneth Bourne became very ill and nearly died. The sickness was sudden and mysterious with the child gasping for air and nearly suffocating. Kenneth survived the attack. That same year Arthur Corning Clark died. Mr. Clark left Mr. Bourne a substantial amount of money and stock holdings in his will. He also left a trust of $1,000,000.00 to his Godson Alfred Severn Bourne which was to be given to him on his 21st birthday. With the newly acquired money and with more freedom in his handling of the Singer business, Mr. Bourne began plans for the construction of his mansion at Indian Neck. This would be the busiest and most dynamic time in Mr. Bourne's life. Following a trip to Europe in the Spring, Mr. Bourne was pushing his endurance to the limits. Overseeing the construction of the mansion, attending to business at Singer, overseeing and attending events at the horse shows, his participation in the races at the yacht club, his duties of director of the Long Island Railroad, traveling and his responsibilities as a husband and father was all too much.

On July 15, 1898 Mr. Bourne was rundown and later in the evening became ill. He was laid up for 2 weeks. When he was feeling better he resumed his duties. In the fall, there would be the horse shows and later preparations would be made for the holiday celebrations. The family was now spending more time on Long Island. With the children now on Christmas vacation it was decided that the family would celebrate the holiday on Long Island with hopes of a white Christmas and sleigh rides across the country roads.

On the morning of Christmas day December 25, 1898, the family enjoyed all the joy and festivities of the holiday at their country home in West Sayville. The mansion was in its final stages of completion. After church service the family would visit their new home in wild anticipation of the first day they would occupy it. The smell of new plaster and newly sawed hardwoods filled the December air within the house. Next year the fireplaces would burn and the family would celebrate the holiday like never before.

It was now time to return to West Sayville. The horses pulling the large yellow carriage were fitted by Mr. Mair with bells. The mile and a half ride back from the mansion was a spirited romp. When the family arrived the servants and cooks had the home in full decoration with many exotic foods and delicacies waiting to be enjoyed. The mood was festive and bright. While the children were enjoying their Christmas toys and presents the festive atmosphere was suddenly shattered when after dinner 7-year-old Kenneth had another attack like the one he had 2 years before. This time the symptoms were much more severe. The child's throat tightened. Soon it was nearly impossible for the boy to breathe. The sounds of the boys suffocating gasps ensued panic and hysteria upon everyone in the house. The doctor was summoned. By the time he could administer help, the boy had died. The official cause of Kenneth's death was listed as "Due to Croup". A modern interpretation of the incident can conclude that there is a strong likelihood the child suffered a food allergy, given the assortment of the unusual delicacies that were served for the celebration. Perhaps one containing peanuts or shellfish.

Christmas celebrations for the Bourne family would be more somber after the death of Kenneth. The following year Mrs. Bourne made a generous cash donation in addition to 75 quarts of ice cream to St. Anne's Church in Sayville. It was the parish in which young Kenneth would attend mass on

Sunday's with his family. In following years Mrs. Bourne and her Daughters would purchase gifts for the children of St. Anne's Church and distribute them personally to the kids on Christmas Day.

The holiday season in 1905 heralded additional celebration. On Sunday November 12, 1905 Arthur Bourne became a proud father. The entire family was exuberant over the birth of Arthur and his wife Ethel's son. The child was given the name of his Grandfather, Frederick. The birth occurred while the Commodore and his wife were duck hunting at their Thousand Island retreat. A year before a new phone system was installed at Indian Neck. After the happy event, the news was given to the Commodore and Mrs. Bourne by wire. The happiness surrounding the baby's birth was short lived. Not long after the delivery, Ethel became seriously ill from complications due to the birth. For nearly a month she suffered from pain and bleeding.

By December 3rd Dr. Hill was summoned to the Oakdale Estate where an emergency surgery had to be performed. Assisted by two other specialists summoned from Manhattan and with the help of a trained nurse the physicians were able to save Ethel's life. Once again, the news was telephoned to the Commodore. Upon learning of the emergency surgery, Mr. Bourne and his wife immediately left the Thousand Island Castle and made tracks back to Oakdale in their touring car. The following day the Commodore arrived back to Indian Neck. Ethel's condition was still guarded. Dr. Hill and the nurse would remain at the estate for continued care during Ethel's recovery.

There was a great deal of anxiety caused by the incident. Marjorie in particular was deeply affected by the illness. Perhaps the most sensitive of all the daughters, Marjorie found her escape in driving fast into Manhattan to her college classes unescorted and with no chauffer. With the death of Kenneth still in their mind, the Bourne family, while deeply concerned over Ethel's illness, was in no way prepared for the unimaginable events which were to transpire this Christmas.

Ethel's condition was so precarious that for a time it was feared there would be no Christmas celebrations at Indian Neck. Happily, Ethel's condition had improved. By the third week into December her recuperation warranted the usual preparations for Christmas. With the promising gift of Ethel's apparent recovery, the holiday promised to be happier than usual. The addition of the infant baby Frederick would ensure even more cause for celebration. The Commodore's namesake gave the entire family a resurgence of optimism for the new year and for the future in general.

Once again, the feelings were short lived. By the closing days of Christmas Ethel's condition began to worsen. She was removed to a sanitarium in Manhattan. Baby Frederick remained at Indian Neck attended to by a wet nurse. On December 24, 1905 Mr. and Mrs. Bourne did their best to make the holiday happy for the children. However, by noon on Christmas day things again suddenly took a turn for the worse. Baby Frederick began having trouble breathing. Like his uncle, a sudden illness had taken over the infant's body and breathing became impossible. Once again, the doctor was summoned. But by the time of his arrival the baby died. As the news of the tragedy spread throughout the estate a feeling of complete shock and sadness prevailed. The flag pole at Indian Neck was set at half-mast out of respect for the Commodore and his family. A quiet wake was held at the estate with only family in attendance. The funeral and internment was at Greenwood Cemetery.

Every Christmas Mr. Bourne would reward the staff at Indian Neck with a cash present. Given the circumstances that surrounded the holiday, such a gesture was not expected, however, Mr. Bourne knew his workers relied on and deserved their Christmas bonus. After the first of the year Mr. Bourne appeared on the grounds of the estate. With a handful of $5 bills he handed each worker a "crisp note" and a handshake thanking them for their hard work. This was just another example of the amount of consideration Mr. Bourne had for others; a quality that endeared him to everyone close to him.

Ethel's condition was still guarded. News of her son's death was not given to her. The family waited for her strength to regain before informing her of the tragic news. The Commodore's wife was chosen to tell her. Having been through the same loss, Mrs. Bourne's participation provided great comfort. By March of 1906 Ethel was well enough to be removed from the sanitarium in Manhattan. She would complete her recovery at the couple's home in the city. Eventually she was well enough to join the re-occupancy of Indian Neck for the beginning of the summer season.

Fifth youngest of the Bourne's six sons seven-year-old Kenneth died on Christmas Day 1898 most likely of a food allergy.

Ethel Bourne

*On Christmas Eve 1905 Ethel Bourne's infant son suddenly
and tragically died. Having gone through a similar tragedy,
her mother-in-law, Emma, helped her through the ordeal.
The incident had a profound effect on her marriage to
Arthur Bourne. The marriage later ended in divorce.*

The Christmas House

THE BOURNE'S TRADITION OF BEING generous to the community during Christmas would continue. In fact, they would become more elaborate and better planned with each passing year. By all accounts it was young Marjorie who was most affected by the events of previous Christmases. She was the youngest daughter and nicknamed Hooley by her family. Marjorie received a great amount of joy in giving out gifts to the children of the community. The traditional celebrations at St. Anne's Church would continue. By Christmas of 1912 the Bourne's tradition of generosity expanded, with Marjorie spearheading the plans. This year the old Fraiser house in West Sayville was used as the site of what was to become an annual Christmas party for all the children in the community. The year before Marjorie attempted to hold a party for the children at the Indian Neck estate. Showing up at the mansion proved to be too intimidating for most the children and their parents. Thus, only 50 children showed up that year.

The Fraiser house was now owned by the Bourne family. It was far less intimidating and a more suitable site for the Christmas celebration. Marjorie was determined to make this years' party more enjoyable. Several weeks prior she posted a notice in the West Sayville Post Office asking children up to age 16 years old to send in their names and ages. With the help of her staff and her brother Howard, Marjorie purchased from local merchants personalized gifts for each child. In a letter written to his daughter May dated December 3, 1912 Mr. Bourne writes *"I can only say that we are all well at home, and the children are busy arranging for Christmas presents for the help at Oakdale"*. At

10:30 on Christmas morning 1912 over 300 children showed up at the house. Dressed as Santa and with the assistance of her brother Howard, Miss Bourne distributed the gifts.

The following Christmas of 1913 a similar event was held. This time the location was changed. The facts revolving around this event were lost to history until the research was done during the writing of this book. In an article dated March 23, 1913 in the Brooklyn Daily Eagle it was reported that the Bourne's former residence located in West Sayville known as *"The famous Widow Molly Inn"* was to be torn down in what the article claims was "The grand march of progress that is sweeping the vicinity of the large Bourne Estate". It is unclear exactly why Mr. Bourne wished to have the house razed. No other article detailing the houses destiny was ever printed. There are several subsequent references that concluded the house was demolished. These include an April 15, 1999 Suffolk County News article and in addition #187 of the 2009 issue of the Titanic Historic Society's News Letter.

The facts are now clear that the house was not demolished and existed until the present time this book was written. Sometime during the summer of 1913 Mr. Bourne had the large house split into sections. A one paragraph article appeared in a 1913 addition of the Suffolk County News stating "Charles Edwards this week finished moving part of the Bourne homestead from Main Street to its present location on Division Street, North of this Village…The building was purchased by Cornelius DeGraff". No mention of where the other portion of the house was moved to. However, the March 23, 1913 article included a photograph of the house. When examined, it was proved to be identical to the authors next door neighbor's house located on what is now known as Dale Drive in Oakdale.

Marjorie had many fond memories of playing with her younger brother Kenneth in the old house. The house was now firmly in place in its new location on what was then known as West Street. By Christmas of 1913 it was still owned by Mr. Bourne and still vacant. Once again Marjorie would put up a posting in the Post Office stating "Come to the last white house on the right-hand side of West Street". This year the tree selected for the party was a large spruce. The tree was magnificently decorated and was unlike anything the 300 youngsters who showed up had ever seen. The party started at 11:00 am and lasted well into the afternoon on that joyous Christmas day. The old vacant house had once again been filled with the sound of children's laughter. A profound sense of joy and good spirits would be a lasting legacy of the old Widow Molly Inn.

Jekyll Island

By 1901 THE BOURNE FAMILY was firmly established in their new home at Indian Neck. A full stable facility, boat house and private docking for their yachts, kennels and automobile garages were on site. Every enjoyment the Bourne's were engaged in was now efficiently organized and easily accessible. Indian Neck was now a haven for the enjoyment for their pleasures. However, Mr. Bourne greatly enjoyed traveling. The arrival of Mr. Bourne's large steam yachts would enable him to include his family and entourage of friends and servants on his trips. Mr. Bourne desired to find a resort in the South where the family could enjoy a vacation for a few weeks away from the chilly winters of Long Island.

A little club resort located off the coast of Georgia was the source of scuttlebutt in the New York Yacht club. Edwin Gould and William Rockefeller had spoken of it often. Frederick Bourne had learned that Jekyll Island was an unpretentious club with members who clung to a philosophy of simplicity; a pleasing contrast to his experiences with the New York horse shows.

Desiring to travel with his wife and daughters, it was advantageous that the Jekyll Island Hunt Club allowed both men and women members. When the Jekyll Island hunt club was founded in 1886 its founders John Eugene Du Bignon and his brother-in-law Newton S. Finny reserved the club's membership exclusively to men. By 1901 women had gained access and once in they played an increasingly significant role in its development. It would evolve from simply an exclusive hunting club into a more family centered community. Activities included carriage driving, bicycling, golf and tennis. However, at its core, the clubs main sporting activity was hunting. Part of its simplistic charm was an emphasis on serving the club members local hunt and fish catches of the day to be included in the food served at the clubs table.

The fact that the Jekyll Island club was only accessible by boat was another factor that made the club desirable to Mr. Bourne and the other club members. Arrivals and departures to and from the Island were strictly controlled. The general public including the press were generally unwelcome unless invited by a club member. It took more than money to become a member of the Jekyll Island Club. People with simply the financial means to become a member were often not accepted. With his extensive knowledge of horses, his skills at hunting and other athletics, Mr. Bourne was an excellent candidate. By 1901 he had secured a membership for himself and his family in the Jekyll Island Club Community.

The Bourne's usually made the 880-mile trip to the island in either January or February. While the club's emphasis was on simplicity, the Bourne's would bring with them an entourage of help including servants, stable workers and mechanics. Earlier trips before 1906 were usually made with either the Delaware or Colonia. Later years the family would often steam down with their yacht the Alberta. Some cargo was secured on the yachts but for the most part a separate rail car was assigned to the Adam's Express Company to convey the necessary horses, carriages and automobiles for use on the island.

Club members included such financially influential people such as the Morgan's, the Rockefeller's and the Vanderbilt's. Given Jekyll Island's seclusion, it is no surprise that the location would become instrumental in an event in history. It was the site where a new policy was made in the financial community. In November of 1910 several influential business and government officials met on Jekyll Island to create a draft for legislation. The policy defined within the legislation would ultimately create the United States Federal Reserve. The legislation was written in response to a financial crisis that occurred in 1907 that is now known as the 1907 Bankers Panic or the Knickerbocker Crisis.

The cause of the panic was primarily due to a time of economic recession coupled with unregulated side trading and stocks. Thus, there was a loss of confidence among bank depositors which ultimately led to numerous runs on banks and trust companies. One of the results of the panic was the downfall of the Knickerbocker Trust Company, an institution where Frederick Bourne was a board member. Additionally, the 1906 earthquake in San Francisco led to an influx of money from New York to San Francisco for reconstruction. Depositors continued to withdraw cash from banking institutions and the panic escalated into a crisis. Recognizing an opportunity, some of the wealthiest men in America stepped in. J.P. Morgan would provide $8.25 Million dollars in loans. John D. Rockefeller provided $10 Million dollars. In addition, other investors provided another $25 Million to allow the banks and trust companies to remain solvent until confidence was restored. The money provided by Morgan, Rockefeller and other investors played a key role in staving off the crisis. However, later they would be the topic of intense scrutiny, being accused of taking advantage of the panic by cashing in on low stock prices and cornering the market of financial institutions.

On the evening of November 22, 1910, the assistant secretary of the United States Treasury along with Republican Senator Nelson W. Aldrich and other financiers met on Jekyll Island to discuss monetary policy and the banking system. The results of the issues discussed during the meeting would ultimately lead to the creation of the Federal Reserve. The meeting on Jekyll Island was extremely secretive. The men convened under the ruse of a duck hunt. Curiously Frederick Bourne's name is not to be found among its participants. By 1914 Mr. Bourne would be elected President of the club, a position that he would hold up until the time of his death. After Bourne's passing Lewis Comfort Tiffany designed a stained-glass window which was commissioned by the executive committee of the club. The magnificent window is located at the west end of Faith Chapel and is entitled "David Set Singers Before the Lord". This wonderful work of art remains until this day on the Island a lasting tribute to Mr. Bourne's legacy.

Frederick Bourne and the Automobile

THE NEW CENTURY USHERED IN a fascination with all things mechanical. No machine exemplified this ideal more profoundly than the automobile.

One of the first automobiles purchased by Mr. Bourne was his 1901 Winton "Bullet." It was a 40-horse power gasoline powered machine, considered by many to be the first "sportscar". Considering that the average automobiles horse power rating now rarely exceeded 20 horse power, Winton's machine was truly exceptional.

Alexander Winton was a Scottish born machinist, engineer and mechanic. In 1868 at the age of 22 Winton settled in Cleveland Ohio. His first venture was in the manufacturing of bicycles, and started the Winton Bicycle Company. Interested in all things mechanical, Winton became fascinated with perfecting and improving the designs for automobiles. The machine began to cut its teeth during the first decade of the 20th century and it would be men like Winton, Ford and many others who would bring the machine to age with the dawn of the new century.

Winton first motorized vehicle was built in 1896. The machine was an amalgamation of design, using bicycle tires and a primitive chain drive. On March 15, 1897 Winton began the Winton Motor Carriage Company. Automobile historians acknowledged Alexander Winton for making the first commercial sale of an automobile in the United States which occurred on March 24, 1898.

It would be in Boston on June 15th 1901 where Frederick Bourne would learn of the Winton's performance during a race held by the automobile club of New England at Brookline Massachusetts. Winton had built and shipped from Cleveland one of his 40 horse power racers to New England. The Bullet was specially built for a wealthy member of the New England Club named Lars Anderson. By November 8, 1901 Bourne would be in possession of his own 40 horse power Winton.

In the summer of that year, during a simmering mid-July heat, Arthur Bourne would lie in bed for two weeks with fever. On July 26, 1901, the automobile house at Indian Neck was nearing completion, and Arthur's health was improving. By August 30th his health had significantly improved. He could often be seen in the new garage, learning what he could about automobiles. With the aid of trained mechanics, he attempted to improve the performance of his own automobile's. His goal was to exceed his father's top speed of 45 miles per hour. There are no records of any success regarding this attempt, but the activity no doubt had a positive effect on his recovery.

"It was reported in the Brooklyn Daily Eagle in an article dated August 30, 1901 by the editor that "We are bound to say, however, that the Bourne's do not use their machines on public roads in such a way as to endanger or annoy people".

Opinions were changed by the Spring of 1902. On May 26, 1902 Arthur Bourne and his newly modified automobile, races from Long Island City to Oakdale ignoring the speed limits of the day. The speed of an automobile through villages was limited to 8 miles per hour and 15 miles per hour on country roads, later this would be changed to 20 miles per hour. These laws were passed through legislation on March 1,1901 by Senator William W. Cocks of Nassau County and was known as the Cocks Law.

A more serious matter occurred early that year on January 21, 1902 when Frederick Bourne was the cause of a runaway horse and wagon. The incident transpired in East Islip when Mr. Bourne was heading to Bay Shore on horse show business. Frederick Bourne's Winton buzzed through town, startling a horse owned by a merchant named Henry Volbracht. The wagon side swiped a curb, causing it to overturn, smashing it to pieces. Both Volbracht and the horse were unhurt, but the wagon was demolished. Having seen and heard the commotion, Bourne turned back, apologized to Volbracht and asked him to send a bill for the damages.

Not long after this accident came another accident reported in a Brooklyn Daily Eagle article dated July 21, 1902. It gives an account of one Mr. Bourne's Chauffeurs driving through Patchogue New York "going like the wind" and startling the driver and passenger of a horse and buggy. The young buggy driver named Gerrodette and his lady companion were so frightened by the automobiles actions that they jumped out of their carriage. The accident was told by a Mr. L.C. Hafner, a New York merchant who owned a home in that town on Bay Avenue. Hafner gave other accounts of automobile infractions far worse, and claimed that one incident was so frightful that "if I had a revolver with me, I certainly would have used it!". The laws governing the registration and licensing of motor vehicles were still in their infancy period. The requirement for vehicle identification in 1902 was limited to the placement of the owner's initials on a plate located in the back of the vehicle. The first license plates issued in the United States were in Massachusetts in 1903. New York did not issue their white on black plate until 1910.

Law enforcement sheriffs and deputy sheriffs oversaw enforcing the speed laws. Speeding automobiles were timed by stopwatches for a quarter mile stretch. The distance was previously surveyed, and through a system of signaling, the watch holding timers can determine an automobile speed to within a fraction of a second (it was alleged!)

The nemeses for the Bourne family would be Sheriff John S. Wells, a brash and outspoken man with a single-minded determination to enforce speeding laws and pacify the concerned sentiments of citizens' complaints. In 1902 Sheriff Wells would fine or arrest members of the Bourne family three times including Frederick Bourne himself on September 19th. In the month of December 1902 Arthur Bourne was arrested and fined twice within the span of four days. His trial was in the town of Babylon on December 5th. It attracted a great deal of attention and drew its court room to its capacity with spectators. The incident occurred during a visit out to Oakdale from New York City on an unusually mild day. Arthur was accompanied by his two sisters and one of Marjorie's pedigree canines. Here they encountered two obstacles to their pleasure in the persons of special officers Bertram F. Mott and his timer Eugene Benjamin who were on the lookout for violators. Mott claimed Bourne's machine traveled over a course of 1/16th of a mile in sixteen seconds. The Bourne's were inclined to plead guilty and pay the $40.00 fine to the magistrate, James B. Cooper. It was at this moment that the incident became a spectacle and highly dramatic with the entrance of John Snedecore, President of the Babylon Automobile Chapter. Snedecore advised Arthur to plead Not Guilty.

Meanwhile outside the justice's residence the Bourne ladies seated in the automobile awaited Arthur's return. News of the arrest traveled fast and a crowd of curious onlookers gathered gawking at the powerful automobile and it's "handsomely gowned and furred occupants." Also at this time the magistrates favorite dog and Miss Marjorie's pedigree engaged in a bark-ing quarrel that escalated in an all-out fight when the pedigree broke free. The fight was short and vigorous. The pedigree held its ground against the street brawler. Members of the crowd took bets as to the winning out-come, however, in the end it was declared a draw. Meanwhile back in the courtroom it was finally decided that the fines would be paid and no appeal would be rendered.

By the close of the first decade of the 20th century, automobile frenzy was in full swing. It was reported in the American Review of Reviews September 1910 page 368 "In the American Confederation it is estimated that there are more than 130,000 automobiles besides some 35,000 mo-tor trucks, delivery wagons, etc. Eight years ago, the number of automo-biles in the United States did not exceed 6,000.

With such a dramatic increase, the demand for better infrastructure was called into play. On January 18, 1903, the New York Times reported of the enactment of the Higbie-Armstrong Law which would provide for state aid to build better roads for automobiles. In 1905 Suffolk County would spend $178,534.00 on road improvements, the largest sum ever in one year until that time.

The composition of roads on the Bourne estate and the surrounding areas on the south shore consisted of crushed oyster shells, provided by the Ockers Oyster Company. The shells provided an excellent surface for the footing of horses, minimizing injuries to their hooves over the more hazardous gravel and stone surfaces. The introduction of the automobile created new problems associated with shelled roads. Tires pulverized the shells and in the dry summer months the dust kicked up by the machines speed covered everything in its path with white powder. It was tracked into homes and was a choking nuisance.

Having done extensive automobile driving through Europe, Frederick Bourne made mention of the fine roads there, especially in Paris. During a July 1907 meeting of Sayville trustees and village club members, it was decided that the most cost effective method to solve the dust problem and improve the local roadways was to oil the roads.

The substance used at the time was known as "Raglan" oil. It was comprised of 20% asphalt and was sprayed by a sprinkler-like device owned by William Cook, one of Islip towns first automobile road contractors. Bourne had used the oily mixture on his estate with some success. After spraying the composition, the road was sanded. The asphaltum road oil and sand composition solved the dust problem but made the road slippery especially directly after its application.

The primitive tires used at the time provided inadequate traction even under the best conditions. Oyster shells when newly laid as pavement provided hazardous traction for automobiles. On August 29, 1904 Marion Bourne and a young friend narrowly escaped with their lives when their chauffeur driven automobile skidded on a newly shelled road in Patchogue, New York. The auto struck the turf embankment after skidding on the shells and turned over, throwing the occupants out. The ladies escaped with only bruises. The chauffer sustained more serious injuries striking the steering wheel with his ribs, cracking them.

On September 14, 1906 Marion Bourne and her sister Marjorie were involved in a more serious wreck. Marion would sustain more serious bruising and lost a front tooth, Marjorie had her finger badly crushed. The incident occurred on the country road midway between Islip and Bay Shore at 5:00 am during an early morning trek into Manhattan. Once again, the car skidded on the shell road, collided with a tree and overturned. Rance, the chauffer, was also cut and bruised. The accident happened less than a quarter mile away from the spot where a driver named Charles W. Lynde had lost his life that past Labor Day, and a little more than a year later from an incident that occurred on August 24, 1905. At that time 3 young men visiting the Bourne estate narrowly escaped being killed when their Pope-Toledo car rolled down an embankment after being struck by a train. It was becoming clear that the fashionable automobile was now showing itself to be a proven killer.

As the demand for improved road surfaces increased the competition for contracts to pave roads with asphalt also escalated. Various compositions of asphalt had been used for decades, however, it was not until the later part of the first decade of the 20th century that machinery to lay it down was perfected. The earliest machines to use hot mixed asphalt (HMA) consisted of shallow iron trays heated over open coal fires. The quality of the mix depended on the skill or the operator. The first practical steam roller was produced in 1867 by a British company named Aveling and Porter. The following year it was exported around the world including France, India and the United States of America. The wide use of asphalt roads would not reach its stride until the late 1930's, long after Frederick Bourne's death. J.S. Helm, President of the Asphalt Institute, noted in 1939 that "Asphalt is an essential material in nearly every form of highway construction and maintenance. In the 4 years from 1934 to 1937, asphalt entered into the construction of more than 4/5th's of the mileage of highways completed under state construction".

mented reference to an automobile turntable on Long Island. The structure is extant but the turntable has been removed.

Bourne garage, Oakdale

Copy neg. by Joseph Adams

In the summer of 1901 Frederick Bourne had this circular garage constructed on his Oakdale Mansion. It could hold up to 20 vehicles. His Daimler, Rolls Royce and French Touring Cars were the finest of their day: Courtesy Manhattan College

The Vanderbilt Cup Races

Frederick Bourne's automotive problems were not limited to himself and his family. Other aristocrats of the gilded era were sharing his concerns with the hazards of driving automobiles. It would not be until October 6, 1906 when a spectator named Kurt L. Gruner of Passaic New Jersey was killed by a racecar during the Vanderbilt Cup Race. The incident occurred in Mineola, the driver, Elliott F. Shepard was driving a 130-horse power Hotchkiss Racer at a speed of 70 miles per hour at a place where the race-course crossed the Long Island Railroad tracks at Krug's corner near Mineola. Mr. Gruner was in a crowd that surged forward. He was struck by the left front corner of Shepard's car with great force throwing him into a telegraph pole crushing his skull and killing him instantly.

Shepard was a relative of Commodore Vanderbilt through the marriage of Vanderbilt's daughter. A year earlier he had also killed a girl during a race in France. Shepard claimed he had not known he hit anyone until he reached the garage at East Norwich. The backlash after the incident was enormous and nearly put an end to the Vanderbilt races. The incident encouraged the men to follow their dreams of creating a private highway for motoring.

This dream would be realized on December 3, 1906 when William K. Vanderbilt Jr. and a group of other officers and directors including Frederick Bourne would begin the planning of the Long Island Motor Parkway. It would be a privately built road through the center of Long Island free of police enforced speed limits. The parkway was constructed of a very costly reinforced concrete with no grade crossings. The road also featured several banked curves which allow the cars to take them at high speeds. Construction of the parkway began with a ground-breaking ceremony in Bethpage on June 6, 1908 with several hundred people in attendance including Frederick Bourne. The May 18th edition of the Brooklyn Eagle had published the next date for the Vanderbilt races to be held in October pending the completion of the course. It was reported that over 2,000 men were employed on the work for the whole summer. Over 11 miles of cement paved Motor Parkway and about 17 miles of existing highway was used.

On the Bourne estate, there was great enthusiasm for the upcoming race. The Bourne's took great pride in having their father on the board of directors for the parkways construction and even greater pride in the stable of automobiles on the Bourne estate and in their garage at 69th street in Manhattan. The 69th street garage housed at least 3 of F.G.'s big gasoline powered autos including his 1905 Clement-Bayard 4 cylinder 24 horse power touring car.

The Long Island Motor Parkway was officially opened on October 10, 1908. The first race was also held that same year. The grandstands were filled with over 5,000 spectators with many thousands more lining the road. It was an international competition with drivers from many nations competing. It would be an American racer names George Robertson driving a Connecticut built racer, a Locomobile, that would prevail as the winner that year.

Frederick Bourne sporting his distinguished beard is seen here foreground center right at the Vanderbilt Parkway opening ceremony. Photo courtesy of William Bellmer and Howard Kroplick.

Vanderbilt Motor Parkway would also host races in 1909 and 1910. During the 1910 race 2 driver mechanics were killed and several spectators were injured. There still were no safe regulations governing crowd control. Newspapers criticized the race organizers for the incident. The backlash was so severe that organizers would abandoned any plans for any additional races on the parkway.

1908 also saw the purchase of Marjorie Bourne's Packard, Model 30 touring car. It boasted a 4-cylinder T-Head 30 horse power engine with a 3-speed gear box, and reliable (for the times) expanding and contracting brakes on the rear wheel hubs. For some time, it had been the ambition of the Bourne siblings to race the south shore express of the Long Island Railroad from the Islip station into the station at Oakdale, a distance of some 5 miles. It would be Marjorie Bourne who would take up the challenge on the evening of June 3, 1908 despite a threat of late rain showers, Marjorie along with her chauffeur drove the Packard to the Islip station and awaited the arrival of the 6 p.m. express.

Bourne, seen here seated at center stage with the white cap, was in attendance at the groundbreaking ceremony of the Vanderbilt Motor Parkway. Photo courtesy of William Bellmer and Howard Kroplick.

"The Race"

WHAT WAS THEN MERRICK ROAD ran parallel to the railroad tracks. For the entire distance both train and automobile can be easily within sight of each other which would add to the drama and excitement of the race. As the train pulled out of the station the automobile had gained some distance against the express. Passenger's on the train soon became aware of the race and crowded to the windows and platforms to watch it. Their excitement was tinged with apprehension when it became evident that Marjorie did not intend to slow down for the train at the Bayard crossing, a little way out of Islip. The road crossed the track there and the automobile raced for the crossing at full speed. The car passed the train and dashed across the tracks only a few feet in advanced of the locomotive.

The race settled down for a run for the next crossing at W. K. Vanderbilt's estate. At the crossing the automobile was passed by the locomotive which by this time had full charge of its own power. However, after the crossing the automobile made a rapid surge on the flats. A wide detour from the tracks gave the train an advantage. By the end of the race the train had pulled into the Oakdale station at about a train length of the automobile.

The news of the race was published in many newspapers and was the talk of the town. By now it seemed to some residents that anyone and everyone was racing over the roads. Sheriff Wells had enough. On the morning of June 8, 1908 George Bourne was arrested in Sayville. Wells charged George with speeding on the main highway road at 40 miles per hour. Later he was arraigned in front of Justice White and paid a fine of $35.00. Sheriff Wells once again claimed he was enforcing the speed laws because of the complaints by local residents.

A year prior to the events in 1908 Sheriff Wells had taken the complaints of speeding into his own hands and organized a posse under the instructions of District Attorney Furman. Sheriff Wells did not have an automobile at his disposal during this time. The District Attorney, also under a lot of pressure from numerous complaints, lent Wells his automobiles to use as one of the first patrol cars in Suffolk County. Wells' posse consisted of his deputies Bedell and Mott in addition, Dr. George W. Clock would act as timer. A decision was made to operate their speed enforcement on Sunday's and the first of the week which were the days the automobile would be available for their use. And so, the stage was set for a confrontation.

A year after the formation of the posse in 1907, Sheriff Wells and his gang were still on the roads enforcing the speed laws. Wells claimed he was enforcing the laws unilaterally without targeting a specific individual or family. However, Frederick Bourne had another opinion. With the recent arrest of his son George, and the well-publicized race involving Marjorie and the locomotive, Fred felt the sheriff "has it in for him" and for other members of his family.

June 16, 1908 was a warm, lazy Sunday morning. Traffic was unusually light on South Country Road on Sunday's, with the exception of church goers and weekend visitors. Sheriff Wells was made aware of a speeding issue by many locals who attended church and witnessed cars buzzing pass the church at alarming speeds. He could think of no better day to gather his band of fellow enforcers together and make a visible presence on the side of the highway not far from the entrance of St. Anne's Episcopal Church in Sayville. Meanwhile Frederick Bourne was on his way to the church to meet up with his family for service when he caught sight of the sheriff and his men "taking it easy by the road side, waiting to see what might develop." What did develop was a confrontation between Frederick Bourne and the sheriff.

Dressed in Sunday finery, Mr. Bourne stepped out of the chauffeured driven 6 cylinder 30 horse power Rolls Royce. He confronted the Sheriff and let him know that under no uncertain terms would he allow the sheriff to use his office to single out and harass his family. He told Wells that he was upset about the publicity over Marjorie's race with the train. He went on the assure the sheriff that he had spoken to his children about obeying the speed laws. However, he was outraged over the fact that George was arrested and that the sheriff was deliberately setting up speed traps near and around his estate. Sheriff Wells denied Mr. Bourne's allegations and then became upset over the fact that Bourne would make such accusations. For a time, the argument became heated and the outcome of the confrontation would yet remain to be seen. It was clear that Mr. Bourne had given the sheriff a "hard call." He reentered the rolls convinced Wells was still "determined to get him."

Sheriff Wells had become a nemesis to all motorists driving in his district because of his strict and some say too strict enforcement of the speed laws. A little more than two months after Bourne's confrontation with the sheriff, Wells' own son Frank, accompanied by his two friends John Hawkins and Jay Brown would be involved in a terrible wreck. The incident occurred on September 22, 1908, just outside of Main Street on South Country Road in West Sayville on the bend in the road just past the old Bourne residence. Hawkins was driving and as the story goes Frank Wells urged Hawkins to "let her out." The automobile's speed could not handle the turn. It lurched into a spin and overturned. The three young men managed to remain in the car pinned underneath. Frank Wells and Jay Brown crawled out but Hawkins remained, his skull fractured. Aided by some passing motorists they managed to extract him from the vehicle. Bleeding badly, he was unconscious. Hawkins was brought to Dr. William Ross and remained in critical condition for days.

News of the accident reached Frederick Bourne the next day. It was told to him by his chauffeur George Metzler. Metzler was a German born mechanic who in 1902 was taken from the Diamler Motor Factory in Germany and brought to the United States to work for Mr. Bourne. On September 12th that same year, Frederick Bourne purchased his first thirty-five horse power Diamler 60 at a cost of $10,000.00. There are other records claiming that the cost of the automobile was $18,000.00. A conversion to today's currency would value the automobile at $250,000.00. Diamler racing cars had already played a dominant role in European automobile racing. Their vehicles were purchased largely based on the virtues of their high performance and reliability. The Diamler 60 thirty-five horse power is regarded by many automobile historians as the first "modern automobile". The chassis had a wide 92.3" wheel base with a low center of gravity which allowed for fast cornering. Originally designed for racing, Mercedes further developed the "60" for transportation over the highway.

When Metzler first came to the U.S. he worked at the garage on 69th Street in Manhattan where Frederick Bourne kept several of his automobiles. It was here when on one evening Metzler became overcome by carbon monoxide gas and was nearly killed. Mr. Bourne sent Metzler out to Long Island to recuperate and was given a home near the estate on West Street. Metzler was one of the most valued workers on the estate. He worked as mechanic, chauffeur, and later superintendent and agent of the Bourne garages.

The irony of the wreck involving Frank Wells and his friends seemed almost laughable had it not been for the seriousness of the incident. The automobile's dangers were becoming clearer. Automobiles of this era were difficult machines to drive. For those who could afford it, a chauffeur was a necessity. Automobiles had to be hand cranked to start, and breakdowns were frequent. A good chauffeur was not only a driver but also required to possess good mechanical skills to keep the machines running. The term chauffer is derived from the French word "Stoker." Many of the early automobiles were steam powered and required the driver to stoke the engine. Early gasoline engines required the cylinder heads to be preheated during cold weather before the engine could be started.

Having had his own children involved in several close calls in automobile accidents, Frederick Bourne would do everything in his power to ensure the safety of his family in their new-found love affair with automobiles.

Frederick Bourne in the driver seat. Photo courtesy of Robert and Patty Mondore.

The Commodore and His Yachts

IT HAS BEEN CLAIMED THAT the concentration of salt and other ions in human blood are remarkably similar to that of the world's oceans. In no case would this be truer than what was running through the veins of Frederick Gilbert Bourne. Within his genealogy were his uncles and cousins who were among the most notable ship builders in Maine. His earliest years in Boston were spent among a sea faring community with which his father was so closely associated. Frederick Bourne was totally immersed within this nautical community from his earliest years. Thus, the young man was destined to have a lifelong love for the sea.

His marriage to Emma Keeler in 1875 would further promote his association with all things nautical. His wife's grandfather was John E. Davidson who was a charter member of the New York Yacht Club. As one of its earliest associates, Davidson was a member of the Regatta Committee during the 1850's. He also frequently acted as judge for the races. Bourne's own association with the New York Yacht Club would not reach its maturity until his nomination as a club member on February 2, 1893.

His first substantial yacht was the Revere. It was a single masted steam powered vessel measuring 48 feet in length. The Revere was built by the ship builders Gustav Hillmann and Samuel Pine of Greenport, New York. Mr. Bourne purchased the vessel in January of 1893 from S. Wilcox. At the time of purchase the Revere was two years old. The Revere was a frequent visitor to the South Shore of Long Island. During the earlier years while living in West Sayville, the Revere was used by the family for excursions in and along the Great South Bay. Frederick Bourne himself often mastered the ship as Captain. The Revere was also on hand for the 8th race for the Americas Cup in 1893 off Sandy Hook New Jersey. This was the golden era of yacht racing and Frederick Bourne would be instrumental in the shaping of its gilded image.

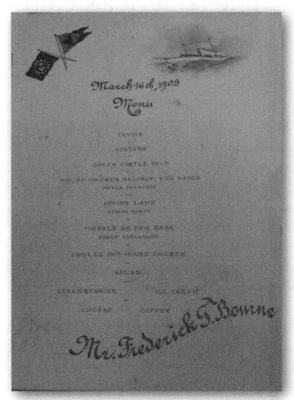

In 1903 Frederick Bourne ascended to the position of
Commodore of the New York Yacht Club. In March of
that year a dinner was given to celebrate the occasion.
The above photograph is an original menu from that dinner.
Photograph courtesy of Dowling College archives.

The America's Cup

THE AMERICA'S CUP RACE DATES to 1851 which incidentally is the same year when Frederick Bourne was born. The trophy, which is affectionately known as the "Auld Mug" was originally award to the Royal Yacht Squadron for a race which took place in that year around the Isle of Wight in England. The Schooner America was victorious in gaining the trophy. It was renamed the Americas Cup after its victor and was donated to the New York Yacht Club under the terms of rules outlined in a document known as the Dead of Gift. The original deed was written in 1852 and was forwarded to the New York Yacht Club on July 8, 1857. Among other things the deed requires each challenging yacht to meet specific requirements to challenge the defending yacht in a match race between the two yachts. The title of the America's Cup has been held by the New York Yacht Club from 1857 until 1983 when the cup was won by the Australian challenger, The Australia II. The Royal Perth Yacht Club had won the title and with it ended the longest winning streak in the history of sports.

In 1893 Frederick Bourne's Revere witnessed one of the great races in the long history of the America's Cup. The New York Yacht Club's centerboard sloop named Vigilant was the defending ship and was pitted against the British challenger Valkyrie II owned by Lord Dunraven, a distinguished member of the House of Lords with an equally distinguished military background. There were many significant design changes on the Valkyrie II giving it a great improvement over its predecessor the Valkyrie I. It had a total length of 117.6' and a displacement of 140 tons. It was constructed with a steel frame, a wood hull and a pine deck. Despite these improvements, the gaff rigged cutter was out matched by the lighter and more maneuverable Vigilant which had a displacement of 138 tons. The Vigilant was owned by a syndicate led by Charles Oliver Iselin. A banker by trade, Iselin was considered one of the greatest yachtsman of his time. His wife Hope was the first woman to serve as a crewmember on an Americas Cup yacht. In the third race of the match the Valkyrie split her spinnaker, crippling the ship and ultimately costing her the second loss in the 3-race match.

Lord Dunraven announced his intentions of again challenging. In a long-winded correspondence, he haggled for changes in the format of the race and for new conditions. Dunraven had constructed a new ship, the Valkyrie III. The American defender for the 1895 race was a sloop of all metal construction consisting of steel, aluminum and bronze. It was owned by William K. Vanderbilt and named the Defender. The race again took place south of the coast of New York in Sandy Hook, New Jersey. Once again Frederick Bourne would be on hand in his Revere to witness the best of 3 match race. In the first fifteen miles of the windward and return race the Defender was victorious. The second race was charted over an equal lateral triangle. The Defender was beaten, but was awarded the race on a foul sustained from the Defender which was hit by the Valkyrie III while jockeying for positions at the start. The Defender's topmast stay had sustained damage from the collision. Lord Dunraven argued the disqualification and declined the third race thus awarding the cup to the Defender.

The America's Cup race of 1895 sparked much controversy. Lord Dunraven accused the defenders of the cup of cheating and in another long-winded letter accused the syndicate owning the Defender as harboring a conspiracy. He claimed Defender has taken on additional ballast and was also guilty of unfair, unsportsmanlike and fraudulent practices. Dunraven had little evidence to support these charges. An investigation followed headed by a blue-ribbon committee that included New York Yacht club members that were well respected. To keep its findings more objective several of the committee members had close ties to England including Naval strategist Alfred Thayer Mahan and banker J. Pierpont Morgan. The committee's conclusions on what is now known as "The Dunraven Incident" entirely exonerated all the Defender's syndicate of any wrong doing. Dunraven's unfounded charges were an embarrassment to the sport and to the club in general. No apology was ever given by Dunraven. After a month of waiting the club expelled him as an honorary member.

The Delaware. Photo courtesy of Manhattan College.

Honor, nobility, respectability, knowledge and fair sportsmanship are characteristics that are the most highly prized in the sport of yacht racing and in the membership of elite yacht clubs in general. It is also no secret that personal wealth plays an important role. To ascend to the title of Commodore one must be in possession of some or all of these qualities. Frederick Bourne possessed all of these attributes. He was honorable in his business practices. Generous in his philanthropic pursuits. He was not born into nobility, however, his wife's grandfather was a charter member of the New York Yacht Club and his great uncles and cousins were well known and respected ship builders. America's young rein in the sport of yachtsmanship was rapidly growing its own members in the noble sect. He had gained respectability as an athlete and horseman and was thoroughly knowledgeable on all things nautical. Most notably by 1901 Bourne was also in possession of great wealth.

In July of 1902 Bourne and his family were abroad in Europe. While in Scotland he purchased from N.R. Stewart of Greenock a steel framed yacht named Maria. She was designed by Mr. G.L. Watson and built at Glasgow in

1896. She had two decks and measured 253' overall. At the time of purchase, she had triple expansion steam engines with a large bore and a 33" stroke. The large and impressive ship had 6 water tight bulk heads and was fitted with the most modern of electric lighting. Designed for the open ocean, the Maria nearly did not make it to the shores of New York. While steaming back from Europe in September the ship encountered a heavy gale 200 miles off the coast of Glasgow. The rough sea pounded the ships deck and hull causing extensive damage. She survived the storm and returned to Europe for repairs. Repaired and refitted, Maria would make her second voyage to the United States successfully. She was renamed Delaware. By 1903 she would be included in the list of vessels belonging to members of the New York Yacht Club. In 1903 Frederick Bourne was elected as Commodore of the New York Yacht Club and his impressive ship Delaware would become its flagship. His fleet captain was named J. D. (Jerrold Kelley). The Colonia was another of Bourne's prize ships. It later succeeded the Delaware as the flagship for the New York Yacht Club during his tenure as Commodore. She had an overall length of 189' and a total tonnage of 259 tons. She was built in Chester Pennsylvania by ship builders Gardener and Cox in 1899. This was the golden era of steam yachts. For the first time power boats would outnumber sailboats within the squadron of ships associated with the New York Yacht Club. Once again, the beginning of the 20th century would witness a transition in transportation relying more on the power of the machine and less on that of nature.

The steam engine with all its advantages also carried with it many dangers during these early years. Modern safety features like low water cutoffs and pressure relief valves were either not invented yet or extremely crude. It was an all too common occurrence for steam boilers to either explode or malfunction due to a lack of incorporation of these safety features. This fact came to horrible reality on the evening of October 14, 1906 when 5 crew members of Frederick Bourne's steam yacht Colonia were killed when the yachts boiler exploded. The tragedy occurred at Oyster Bay Cove.

Earlier that day at 11 a.m. Mr. and Mrs. Bourne were aboard the Colonia, arriving to Oyster Bay from Manhattan. Upon arrival Mrs. Bourne departed from the ship and left with some guests via automobile on a trip to Indian Neck in Oakdale. The Commodore drove back to Manhattan leaving the crew on board. John Leonard, the chief engineer, accompanied by James Southard the fireman and 3 stokers James O'Hara, Alfred Grippe and John Edwards. The men enjoyed a hearty dinner on board. Afterwards they started down into the engine room. There are two accounts of what transpired next. The Brooklyn Daily Eagle and the New York Tribune reported the boiler exploded, resulting in massive damage to Colonia's engine room and upper decks. The New York Times reported a more accurate description of the events. While the 5 men were working on Colonia's boiler a main steam pipe ruptured which immediately filled the small engine room compartment with incredibly hot pressurized steam which immediately scalded the men. The remaining crew went to rescue the men after the intense heat from the steam had subsided. The injured men were transferred to the Long Island Railroad Station where after some delay a special car took them to Nassau Hospital in Mineola. Upon hearing the news Mr. Bourne drove from Manhattan to Nassau Hospital at lightning speed ignoring all speed restrictions. Upon arrival at the hospital Mr. Bourne ordered that no expense be spared to save the men. It was too late for Southard and Grippe who died upon arrival. The remaining 3 men also perished soon after. The following January Frederick Bourne donated $6,000.00 to Nassau Hospital for the dispensary and lab building. This generosity would greatly aid in helping others in the future.

On June 13th of that same year the Colonia sustained damage after striking the steam Yacht Viking while in the basin of West 86th Street in Manhattan. The Colonia and the Delaware for all their grandeur seemed to carry with them a stroke of bad luck. After the tragedy on the Colonia Bourne abandoned the cruise to South America on which the Colonia was being prepared for. The ship remained laid up in a Hoboken New Jersey boat basin. She was repaired, but never again used by the Commodore. On September 23, 1909, the Colonia was sold to a group of brothers from Canada. She was delivered to her new owners at a point near the Bourne Castle in the Thousand Islands.

Prior to the 1906 tragedy, in February 1905 the Commodore's former flagship the Delaware sustained substantial damage when she caught fire while moored next to the Colonia in the 15th Street boat basin in Hoboken New Jersey. The Delaware was being fitted for an extended cruise to the West Indies in March. The fire started at 8:30 in the evening. The two vessels had a crew of about a dozen men on board to look after them. By the time the fire alarm was sounded the fire had gained considerable strength. A fleet of tugs from the Erie Lackawanna Piers responded to the alarm marshalling their strength in conjunction with the Hoboken Fire Department. Ice surrounding the harbor and the basin was formidable. The tugs butted through the ice and gained ample proximity to the ships in order to administer their streams onto the flames.   The Delaware sustained the brunt of the fires merciless damage. The blaze could be seen for miles and lit up the winters sky. Despite the firefighter's herculean efforts, the ships – especially the Delaware had sustained profound damage, mainly to her upper decks which were completely destroyed. Mr. Bourne sometimes wondered if the laws of providence were against him and his family. In a letter addressed to his daughter May dated January 8, 1913 Mr. Bourne addressed this issue. He was explaining a near disaster that he believed the family had avoided regarding an ocean voyage they were about to embark on. In the letter, he explains...

> *"Beginning last Friday morning we had a terrific gale here blowing up to 90 miles an hour. The river was quite a site, and at Oakdale all the meadows were covered and the water was lashed into a seething foam. The family were very much pleased to feel they were not aboard the George Washington which was to sail on Saturday morning at 10:00, but was sorry to miss the Adriatic which left yesterday, only to run a ground in a thick fog down the lower bay, and this morning the fog is still with us. I merely mention these little details to show that sometimes luck does go with the family, and the only wet blanket on the whole thing is that we have to miss seeing you."*

Back at Indian Neck the large flagpole which was formerly the original main mast on the Delaware was lowered to half-mast in honor of the damaged ship. The mast was installed a few years earlier when it was removed from the ship.

In this photograph taken aboard the Delaware, Thomas Lipton is seen chatting with Alice Roosevelt, the President's daughter while Frederick Bourne attends to business in the background. Photograph courtesy of Dowling College archives.

By February 1906 the Delaware was refitted and repaired and sold to Adam W. S. Cochrane. She was renamed the Diana. The Diana was later purchased by C. Ledyard Blair, a member of the New York Yacht Club and the Jekyll Island Club. Blair later became Commodore of the New York Yacht Club with the Diana as its flagship. During World War I Blair gave the yacht to the U.S. Government which used it as part of its fleet.

After the loss of the Delaware and the Colonia Bourne's next most majestic yacht would be his Alberta. The Alberta was built in 1896 by G.L. Watson in the prominent ship yards of Scott and Company at Greenock Scotland. She was a virtual twin ship of the Delaware. Mr. Bourne loved the Delaware, but wanted to separate himself from the misfortune that surrounded her. The Alberta was everything the Delaware was in every way without the stigmas associated with her. At the time of her construction the Alberta was considered by many to be the greatest steam yacht afloat. The Alberta's original name was the Margarita. At 278' long and with a total weight of 1,322 tons she was slightly larger than the Delaware. The Margarita's original owner was A.J. Drexel. In Harry Brown's book The History of American Yachts and Yachtsman, designer G.L. Watson admits...

"The Margarita is his masterpiece and that he gave more thought to her than any steam yacht he has every designed (page 79)."

The Alberta. Photo courtesy of Philip Selvaggio
private collection.

At trial the yacht had shown a speed of 13 knots. She had 10 watertight compartments. Her decks were constructed of steel covered with panel teak. She had two bridges, one for navigating purposes and the other for guests. The Margarita was a very comfortable ship. She had a total of three decks. Her drawing room extended the full width of the ship and was furnished in pure Luis XV style. The library was furnished in empire style. The dining room was Chippendale with woodwork of carved Spanish mahogany. The ceiling over the dining area was domed with leaded glass. Also, included on the ship was a smoking room walled with oak panels. The ship was fitted with over 800 electric lights that were powered by an electric generator, which in turn was powered by the ships engines. The Margarita was an ideal representation of the golden age of steam yachts. A model of elegance, extravagance and speed. It was a new age and a new century. Watson's masterpiece would personify all that this new age would represent. A.J. Drexel would eventually sell the Margarita. For several years, she was later owned by King Leopold of Belgium during which time she was named Clementina.

Commodore Bourne purchased the ship in 1914. On July 3, 1914, the ship arrived in New York from Venice, Italy at which time she was renamed the Alberta. On the trip over she was commanded by Captain A.H. Curtis who was one of the leading yacht masters of Europe. With the memories of the Titanic disaster, and the troubled trip overseas experienced by the Diana in 1902, Mr. Bourne wanted the best captain money could buy to assure that the Alberta would make a safe and uneventful trip to the United States.

In the Spring of 1918 Bourne took his last extensive trip overseas. Joining him with his yacht Diana was C. Ledyard Blair. The last leg of the trip was bound for Russia, where Bourne would rescue the few remaining American executives working at the Singer plant located there. In the prior year of 1917 the American council at Irkutski Siberia endeavored to prevent nationalization of the Singer Company by the newly formed Soviet government. Their efforts were unsuccessful. In fact, the only American company to escape nationalization was the International Harvester Co. which did so through a special decree by Lenin himself. The loss of assets to the Singer Company by the nationalization policy totaled over $84 million dollars. Bourne was a long-time friend of the Russian people and was successful at negotiating permission to bring the Alberta to port and pick up the Singer executives. It would be his last and most noble yacht excursion and another example of how Mr. Bourne used his money and resources to help others.

Thomas Lipton

ONE OF FREDERICK BOURNE'S CLOSEST friends was Thomas Lipton. In 1899 Lipton also began a close but competitive relationship with the New York Yacht Club when he entered his yacht the Shamrock II as a challenger for the America's Cup. Like Bourne, Lipton was a genius at promoting his business interests. He would use his participation in the races to promote his products. Lipton would challenge for the cup five times between 1899 and 1930, and in the time between his first challenge and until Bourne's death in 1919, the men would leave a legacy of respectability and honor to the sport.

Like Bourne, Lipton's beginnings in life were very humble. His parents were of Irish decent, Thomas and Francis Lipton immigrated from Ireland to Glasgow, Scotland during the time of the great Potato Famine in 1845. Thomas Jr. was born in a tenement house on Crown Street in Glasgow. In time his parents gathered up enough money to lease a small shop on 13 Crown Street where they began in a retail provisions trade. Unlike Frederick Bourne young Thomas did not have a great fondness for books or for formal education in general. However, like Bourne he did have a natural affinity for business and most importantly for the power of advertisement and self-promotion. He also was an incredibly hard worker with seemingly unlimited energy in his broad shouldered six-foot frame. In time, he used his skills to open a string of Lipton Markets, first in Glasgow and eventually throughout Scotland.

Lipton stores were successful because he cut out the middleman by creating a thrifty distribution system and passed on his savings to his customers. By the late 1880's tea drinking was becoming all the rage in Britain. Lipton used his same marketing strategies to corner the tea trade. He did extensive testing with tea blends, and went as far as to blend each tea to best suit the chemical properties of the local waters found throughout Great Britain. His formula created the finest tasting tea to be found for the price. He made further innovations in tea packaging, putting his tea leaves in measured packets. This assured customers they were getting the exact weight and measure of tea with every purchase. His customers loved the taste of his tea and the consistency of his packaging. Soon Lipton Tea was world renowned, and hailed as the finest tea at its price. With the success of his markets and his tea, by the 1890's Lipton was a multimillionaire.

Like Frederick Bourne Lipton used his wealth to indulge in his passions, the greatest of which was sailing. Lipton's debut as a yachtsman took place when his was 11 years old when he resolved to build a model with his own hands. He used an old gully knife to carve the hull of a boat out of a massive lid from an old wooden chest. Afterwards he made a mast and bow sprit with rigging. From a sturdy piece of paper he constructed a sail. Near Crown Street was a field where there was a huge hole which was a relic from an old brick making operation. It was filled with water and on this muddy pond Lipton launched his first yacht. He named the humble vessel The Shamrock!

Lipton's happiest boyhood days were spent by the riverside with his wheelbarrow. He would visit the steamers coming to shore on the Clyde River. He would purchase small shares of their cargo to sell in the family store. Wondering over the wharves and docks he began to study the different steamers and crafts. He purchased a map of the world and found great delight in tracing the voyages of the ships that he came to know. In this way, he developed a passion for ships, shipping and everything connected to the ocean; it was a passion that would never leave him. By the time he grew to manhood and with his fortune firmly in place Lipton would ply his passions within his trade.

In 1898 Lipton purchased a Clyde built 1,240-ton steam yacht. The ship was originally named the Aegusta, later he renamed it the Erin. She was 260 feet long, with a beam of approximately 30 feet and usually carried a compliment of 40 men. The ships staff included 2 stewards from Ceylon who often dressed in exotic native outfits festooned in traditional Cingalese head dress.

Guests would agree that the men were the most able and gracious workers aboard. Lipton was now acquiring most his tea from Ceylon which is now known as Sri Lanka. The Erin was one of the most elegant yachts of its time. It included a central art salon containing paintings of both watercolor and oils. It also included photographs of crown heads, princes and princesses signed with autographs and messages of thanks and appreciation. The main deck included a music room. Also, complimenting the Erin was a wine tasting area with 5,000 bottles of wine and a vast assortment of scotch whiskey some of which was of Lipton's own brand.

Lipton was determined to win the America's Cup not only for the glory of bringing the prize to the United Kingdom, but also for the notoriety and the publicity the race would bring towards his business interests. The Erin would also be used to escort his Shamrock challengers across the Atlantic for the race. In 1903 Lipton brought over his Shamrock III to race in a challenging match against Oliver Iselin's Herreshoff built sloop Reliance. The Reliance was larger and somewhat ungainly but was very fast. She proved herself handily in the hands of racing captain Charlie Barr in an almost no contest win against the Shamrock III. The race was nearly postponed due to a tragic accident that occurred during the Shamrock III's sail over to the states. The ship was severely damaged in a squall shortly after leaving the harbor of Weymouth, England. One crewman was thrown overboard and drown. Sir Thomas himself was nearly killed as he was knocked down a hatchway. The hull of the Shamrock III was not damaged, but her mast and other rigging was severely damaged or lost. She was towed back to Southampton, England for repairs that cost over $25,000.00. Upon hearing of the accident, Commodore Bourne sent a telegram to Lipton conveying his sympathy to his friend and offered a postponement to the race. Afterward Lipton replied with sincere thanks and declined the offer saying the Shamrock III "would be ready to fill her engagements as scheduled".

In his autobiography, Lipton states:

I am often told that I am the world's greatest optimist...There is something buoyant and healthy in being an optimist. It is because of my optimism that I have gone through life smiling".

He was also a man who refused to look backwards at the troubles he experienced. It was not that he was uncaring, but rather it was counterproductive and fettered the mind in its ability to think clearly. This was a notable trait he shared with Bourne. During their discussions over the races early on when Bourne was Vice Commodore of the New York Yacht Club, the two men spent a good amount of time together. In the summer of 1902 Bourne traveled to Southampton, England along with fellow Republican, Lieutenant Governor Timothy L. Woodruff as guests of Thomas Lipton on board his steam yacht Erin. Lipton's American guests were journeying to be on hand for the coronation of King Edward VII and Queen Alexandra.

On July 5, 1902, the men hosted a charity dinner which was given to feed the poor throughout the London area. At the behest of the King, Lipton organized the feast which was to feed some 500,000 of London's poor. The dinners were given in about 400 halls in various parts of the district of London. The most noteworthy of which was the dinner at Fulham, which under the personal supervision of Lipton some 14,000 were fed around 2 ½ miles of tables. Plates of roast beef, bread and commemorative glasses of beer were ceremoniously doled out by Lipton, Bourne and the Lieutenant Governor. The Prince and Princess of Wales were also in attendance along with many other foreign dignitaries. It is noteworthy to mention the commendable behavior of London's poor during the event. Despite the free beer, no major incidents were reported. In fact, the only trouble occurred a week before on June 27[th,] when in several smaller towns groups of "hobos" demonstrated by setting fires and breaking windows when it was reported that the dinners would be delayed! Notice of the possible delay was given on the account of the 59-year-old King's health. Overweight and fond of large meals and cigars, the King was suffering from an abdominal cyst. Unable to attend the celebrations personally, the King insisted the dinners were to commence as planned no doubt to stave off additional rioting.

The massive dinner was one of the largest in history. Bourne had brought the Lieutenant Governor for some positive publicity to mend fences with the new Republican party within the state. Woodruff was an ardent businessman. A director of the Merchants Exchange National Bank, a graduate of Yale and a good friend of Theodore Roosevelt with whom he served under briefly as Lieutenant Governor before Roosevelt's nomination as Vice President in 1900. Woodruff was also somewhat of a Forest Gump like personality known for his wide variety of interests and skills from an arbiter of fashion, to ping pong expert. However, as of late he was pouring oil on the troubled waters of the waring Republican factions in Brooklyn. As a favor to his fellow Republicans, Bourne brought Woodruff with him to England to allow time for his party to prepare a proper dressing for the fruit bowl of New York politics; a mix in which Frederick Bourne had no profound interest personally.

The summer trip of 1902 would cement the friendship between Bourne and Lipton. Bourne would make several more trips to Europe to visit his friend including a two-month trip in February of 1913. The following year in March of 1914 Lipton would visit Bourne on his estate in Oakdale to discuss yet another attempt at challenging for the America's Cup with his Shamrock IV. Earlier in that same year Lipton visited in July where again he was received warmly by the Bourne family and the community.

On December 27, 1912 Lipton spent the weekend after Christmas at the Bourne estate. Bourne gave Lipton a tour of the newly constructed Telefunken Wireless Plant in West Sayville and later visited the oyster plant of the Blue Point Oyster Company where they sampled a plate of the finest oysters in the world at the time. During a dinner at the New York Press Club that Friday evening, the British yachtsman said "it begins to look as if you would see Tommy Lipton with his racing flag off Sandy Hook in 1914".

The New York Yacht Club's boat was named Resolute. R.W. Emmons II would be its captain. Frederick Bourne was one of several men funding her construction. However, the hand of fate would reach out and cast away any dream of victory that year for Lipton. On August 7th, the Erin would receive word by wireless that England had declared war on Germany. The race was canceled. Lipton would not see another challenge until 1920. The two men kept in correspondence through the war years up until Bourne's death on March 9, 1919.

Singer Castle

By 1903 Bourne had secured his position as Commodore of the New York Yacht Club. He was in possession of several of the clubs most magnificent yachts, including its flagship the Delaware. The large steam yachts with their powerful engines allowed Mr. Bourne and his family to cover great distances in luxury and speed. Indian Neck would always be home for the Bourne family, but the heat and stifling humidity of Long Island summers were unbearable during these pre-air-conditioned times. Remembering summers spent with the Clark family in Cooperstown, Mr. Bourne thought it would be a good idea to build a summer hunting lodge upstate.

In a region on the St. Lawrence Seaway in Upstate New York is an area commonly referred to as the Thousand Islands. The average high temperature in this area for the month of July is 70 degrees. The comfort index for the region scores 14 points above the national average, this fact Mr. Bourne could only know in his day by frequenting the area on excursions up the St. Lawrence via the Hudson River. A series of locks and canals designed in 1871 allowed transit of moderate sized vessels of up to 186' long and 44' 6" wide through the sea way. Mr. Bourne made good use of the system. In 1902 Bourne purchased one of the most desirable islands in the area for the construction of his new lodge. Dark Island as it was known was purchased for $5,000.00. In 1903 Bourne once again hired Earnest Flagg to design the structure in the vision Bourne had imagined. The scale and grandeur of Bourne's idea even took his family by surprise. During their trips to Europe the Bourne's were impressed by European castles. His stay in England with

Lipton in 1902 further nurtured Bourne's belief that Flagg's design for the new lodge should be a castle. Additionally, during this time both Mr. Bourne and Earnest Flagg were reading a book by Sir Walter Scott. The title was Woodstock or the Cavalier. It is a story of a gallant old cavalier Sir Henry Lee and his loyalty to his fugitive King, Charles II of England. Scott's book was imaginative and romantic. The impetus on which the Bourne's Singer Castle would be created.

While Flagg was designing the structure, the building was referred to as "The Towers" a title that accurately described its design. Construction on Flagg's five story masterpiece began in 1903. Granite from nearby Oak Island was quarried by over 90 stone masons who worked year-round on its installation. The first building to be completed was the North Boat House. The structure would provide safe shelter for Mr. Bourne's vessels during his trips to the site to oversee its construction. The magnificent stone castle also had other structures built in conjunction to the main house which would complement its functionality and design. These included a caretaker's cottage, ice house, two large boat houses and a clock tower. The clock for the clock tower was not installed until twenty years after the castle was built. Marjorie admired the clock Mr. Bourne had installed at the Indian Neck property in 1912. Having inherited the castle after Mr. Bourne's death, in the 1920's she had a similar clock installed on the castles clock tower. Its four twelve-foot clock faces were four feet larger than those located at Indian Neck. Both movements were designed by the E. Howard Clock Company of Boston. The sound of the Westminster chimes undoubtedly reminded Marjorie of her father and of the happy years they spent together at Indian Neck.

In 1905 the construction was completed. The $500-thousand-dollar castle boasted twenty-eight rooms, thirteen fireplaces, stone spiral stairways, Spanish red tile roofs and copper gutters. One of the most charming features is the large front tower or turret. Housed within the turret on its five floors were a private office, exotic round bathrooms and the castles dungeon!

The Final Years

FREDERICK BOURNE CONTINUED TO HAVE an active lifestyle well into the second decade of the 20th century. Mr. Bourne was enjoying a semi-retired life being free of most of the responsibilities at Singer, serving now as an advisor on its Board of Directors. Mr. Bourne and his family were spending more time at their home in Oakdale and on the St. Lawrence River in their marvelous castle. In addition, they continued to travel to Europe extensively, usually during the month of May.

It was on May 12, 1911 when Mr. and Mrs. Bourne's daughter May married Ralph B. Straussburger who was a graduate of the Naval Academy and a former Navy Lieutenant as well as a member of the New York Yacht Club. The wedding took place at St. John's Church in Wickham England. A week before the wedding the young couple and Mr. and Mrs. Bourne drove throughout the English countryside touring castles and enjoying the company of friends and associates.

Two years later Mr. Bourne returned to England to visit his friend Thomas Lipton to discuss the details of the upcoming Americas Cup Challenge. On May 21, 1913 Mr. Bourne returned from England. On May 21st, the Commodore would suffer an attack of acute indigestion accompanied by severe stomach pains. Mr. Bourne was confined to bed for much of the month of June. In a letter addressed to his daughter May dated July 6, 1913 Mr. Bourne wrote:

"Owing to a slight setback in my usual vigorous health, I was compelled to give up fishing this year and remain in Oakdale being on Doctor Hills restricted diet until the 1st".

By July he was feeling well enough to journey to their home on Dark Island where again he wrote his daughter May stating that his illness was:

"Due to indiscretion in eating and going ahead too fast after my trip abroad, I am in good shape now and have gained four pounds since leaving Oakdale July 1ˢᵗ. Fresh air up here is a tonic with nothing to do but sit still and read and lie down all day and night. With diet restricted and your mother and Marjorie watching me, how can I help but improve."

The illness took strength from Mr. Bourne that would never fully return. He was not a man accustomed to a sedate lifestyle. However, with his health deteriorating, he was forced to do so and for the remaining six years of his life his activity level was diminished. Although weakened, Mr. Bourne did recover enough to take care of business. In fact, the following year of May 12, 1914 Mr. Bourne filed suit against the Blue Point Oyster Company in an effort to get the company to relocate their oyster facility at the foot of West Street in West Sayville New York. Mr. Bourne's complaint was that the facility blocked access to the shore front. He asserted that by blocking access to the bay, Mr. Ockers, the owner of the company, was denying the community of West Sayville with access to the bay. West Street was then and continues to be the only public road allowing access to the bay in that area. Mr. Ockers was opposed to the request and thus a lawsuit was filed against him. Mr. Bourne also had a personal issue with the oyster house issue. His daughter Florence's new home was constructed very nearby. The suit dragged on until the end of December of 1915 when the appellate court decided in favor of Mr. Bourne.

The world was changing by the beginning of 1915. Income tax was now in effect. The public pressured politicians to put more scrutiny on the wealthy to contribute to national causes through taxation. The glimmer of the gilded age was rouging. The new post Victorian error heralded changes in the global economy due in part to what was known then as "The Great War". With what is known today as "World War I", traveling abroad became increasingly unsafe. The spring trips to Europe were suspended. Despite this, friends from Europe including Thomas Lipton still frequented as guests at the estate in Oakdale. The men would spend many hours on Mr. Bourne's yacht

Alberta talking over old times and Sir Thomas' exploits with his Shamrock series of watercraft and his quest to win the Americas Cup Trophy. Lipton regarded Mr. Bourne as a good friend and was always given the finest of treatment when visiting the Oakdale estate.

In April of 1916 Alexander Mair had an attack of acute appendicitis. On the 18th of April Mr. Bourne's trusted friend died. During this time, Mr. Bourne was also attending to his wife Emma who was suffering from the effects of cancer. On the 31st of August 1916 Emma Bourne, a devoted wife and mother, passed away at their home in Oakdale. The funeral was held at Indian Neck and was private with only the Bourne's family and a few close friends in attendance.

With the death of his wife, Mr. Bourne was deeply saddened. His spirits were further diminished by the news of his younger son Howard's illness in 1918. In the fall of 1916 Howard was not feeling well. Like his father, he also had a great love for the sea. He believed that an extended ocean voyage would have a profound positive effect in his quest to regain good health. He started on an extended trip through Asia, Australia and New Zealand. Accompanying him was the family physician Dr. Campbell. Initially the fresh sea air was doing Howard well and with Dr. Campbell attending, Howard's spirits and his health were improving. Unfortunately, during this time, the now infamous flu pandemic of 1918 was beginning to make itself known. The pandemic would cover the world from the Pacific Islands, the Artic and all continents. Over 500,000,000 people globally would be affected by the H1 and N1 virus. It is estimated that the virus was responsible for killing between 3 to 5 percent of the world population in 1918. The pandemic is noted as being one of the deadliest natural disasters in human history. While in Auckland New Zealand 25-year-old Howard Bourne became ill with the flu. As the fever and illness progressed pneumonia set in. On November 14, 1918 Dr. Campbell sent word to the family in Oakdale that Howard had died.

After Howard's death Mr. Bourne's health began to rapidly deteriorate. His bout with digestive troubles became more frequent and severe. He lost weight and his energy level had diminished. Mr. Bourne would be under the care of his other trusted physician Dr. George S. King. After examination, Dr.

King had concluded with the diagnoses of stomach cancer which at its current state was inoperable. Having seen his wife through cancer, Mr. Bourne knew what was expected. Soon after, the Commodore was confined to his bed. During the last few days Dr. King would remain with Mr. Bourne at his home in Indian Neck. At one point as Dr. King was sitting with him at his bedside Mr. Bourne said:

> *"I've been thinking, that by merely touching my finger to that bell I can have anything in the world a man could wish for and yet the only thing I really desire is a glass of water and now I know that even if I could have it, it would cause me distress".*

One source of comfort during his final days would be listening to his daughters play his favorite musical selections on the organ. On his last day March 9, 1919 Dr. King had told him that death was close. Mr. Bourne asked for his children to come in and he said his last goodbyes. Before they left he asked that they play for him the song "The End of a Perfect Day", and then until he slipped away "Abide by Me". Mr. Bourne thanked Dr. King for staying with him. He then wished several of his closest servant's goodbye and at 3:00 on that Sunday afternoon the Commodore closed his eyes and as Dr. King wrote *"His spirit soared outward on the wings of music".*

The funeral service for Mr. Bourne was held at Indian Neck at 11:00 am on the following Wednesday. Close friends and business associates from New York City arrived at the train station in Oakdale at 10:30 on a special train. Among the guests in attendance were Cornelius Vanderbilt, John Pierpont Morgan and William Rockefeller. Also, paying tribute were 16 members of the boys' choir from St. John the Devine. The cathedrals organist played Mr. Bourne's favorite selections. Bishop Greer of the Protestant Episcopal church conducted the service. At 2:00 pm another special train was waiting at the Oakdale station to take Mr. Bourne to his final resting place in the family mausoleum at Greenwood Cemetery in New York. Mr. Bourne's casket was constructed of heavy oak as a tribute to the namesake of his beloved adopted town. The casket was covered with a blanket of violets. Hundreds of floral tributes were delivered to Indian Neck from friends, a true testament to the revere, respect and love that was felt for this beloved man.

This magnificent pipe organ was installed in the music room at the Indian Neck Estate on January 23, 1909 by the Aeolian Pipe Organ Company. At the time it was the largest privately owned pipe organ in the world containing 101 speaking stops. The price of the organ was reported as $50,000.00. It replaced a smaller instrument which was installed on April 7, 1899.

SELECTED BIBLIOGRAPHY

Alpern, Andrew. The Dakota: A History of the World's Best Known Apartment Building. New York Princeton Architectural Press 2015.

Bissell, Don. The First Conglomerate: 145 Years of The Singer Sewing Machine, Audenreed Press 1999, Brunswick, ME.

Brown, Harry. The History of American Yachts and Yachtsmen. New York 1901, Spirit of the Times Publishing Co.

Hale, Philip H. The Book of Live Stock Champions. Saint Louis Mo, 1912. Published by Philip H. Hale (Pg. 182, 320).

Havemeyer, Harry W. Along the Great South Bay. Mattituck, New York: Amereon House, 1996.

Holliday, Diane & Kretz, Chris. Images of Oakdale, Charleston, SC. Arcadia Publishing, 2010

King, George S. M.D. Doctor on a Bicycle. New York: Rinehart & Company, Inc., 1958.

Lipton, Thomas. Lipton's Autobiography. New York: Duffield and Green, 1932.

McCash, June Hall. The Jekyll Island Cottage Colony. Athens, Georgia: University of Georgia Press, 1998.

Mondore, Robert and Patty. Singer Castle. Charleston, SC: Arcadia Publishing, 2005

Mondore, Robert and Patty. Singer Castle Revisited. Charleston, SC: Arcadia Publishing, 2010.

Murphy, Thomas W. Jr. The Wedding Cake House: The World of George W. Bourne. Kennebunk, Maine: Published by: Thomas Murphy, 1978.

Rousmaniere, John. The New York Yacht Club: A History 1844-2008. New York: New York Yacht Club 2009.

Semsch, O.F. A History of the Singer Building Construction. New York Shumway & Beattie, 1908.

The American Hackney Horse Society. The American Hackney STUD Book Vol. I. New York: John Polhemus Printing Company, 1893.

Weber, Nicholas Fox. The Clarks of Cooperstown. New York; Alfred A. Knopf, 2007.

Clark, Alfred Corning. Lorentz Severin Skougaard: Asketch, Mainly Autobiographic. New York: G.P. Putnam's Sons, 1885.

****All articles written by newspapers staff writer
unless otherwise mentioned****

"Bourne and Sheriff Met." <u>The Brooklyn Daily Eagle</u> Brooklyn, New York June 16, 1908, Page 1.

"Sheriff's Son in Auto Crash." <u>The Brooklyn Daily Eagle</u> Brooklyn, New York September 22, 1908, Page 5.

"Biggest Show of Automobiles." <u>The New York Times,</u> New York January 17, 1904, Page 15.

"Bourne Auto Wrecked." <u>The Brooklyn Daily Eagle</u> Brooklyn, New York September 14, 1906, Page 1.

"Bourne Favors Macadam." <u>The Brooklyn Daily Eagle</u> Brooklyn, New York January 4, 1906, Page 1.

"E. F. Shepard's Auto Kills Spectator." <u>The New York Times</u>, New York October 7, 1906, Page 3.

"Enforce Speed Law Say Long Islanders." <u>The Brooklyn Daily Eagle</u> Brooklyn, New York July 21, 1902, Page 14.

"George Bourne Arrested." The Brooklyn Daily Eagle June 8, 1908, Page 18.

"Village Club Active (Road Construction)." The Suffolk County News Sayville, New York July 26, 1907, Page 3.

"A Double Fatality." The Suffolk County News Sayville, New York December 29, 1916, Page 1.

"Frederick G. Bourne's Son Arrested." The Brooklyn Daily Eagle Brooklyn, New York December 1, 1902, Page 5.

"Mr. Bourne's Auto Overturned." The Suffolk County News Sayville, New York September 2, 1904, Page 2.

"Bourne Again Fined $40.00." The Brooklyn Daily Eagle Brooklyn, New York December 5, 1902, Page 12.

"Vanderbilt Cup Race-Twenty Cars had Perfect Scores." The Brooklyn Daily Eagle Brooklyn, New York, August 13, 1910, Page 19.

"Miss Bourne's Motor in Race with Train." The New York Times, New York June 4, 1908, Page 1.

"Bourne Girls Injured." The Brooklyn Daily Eagle Brooklyn, New York September 15, 1906, Page 1.

"F.G. Bourne's Auto Upset." The Brooklyn Daile Eagle Brooklyn, New York August 29, 1904, Page 1.

"Bourne's Hastening Home – Fast Auto is Whirling Them Across the State to Bedside of Mrs. A.K. Bourne, at Oakdale." The Brooklyn Daily Eagle Brooklyn, New York December 3, 1905, Page 1.

"Fine Horses on Long Island." <u>The Brooklyn Daily Eagle</u> Brooklyn, New York. December 8, 1895, Page 20.

"Auto Causes Smash-up." <u>The Brooklyn Daily Eagle</u> Brooklyn, New York. January 21, 1902, Page 20.

"Honoring A Prominent Summer Resident." <u>The Suffolk County News</u> Sayville, New York March 22, 1890, Page 1, Column 1.

"What's in a Name." (Chicken Street) <u>Suffolk County News</u> Sayville, New York March 22, 1890, Page 1, Column 1.

"A Big Job." <u>Suffolk County News</u> Sayville, New York March 22, 1890, Page 1, Column 2.

"Greenville News." <u>Suffolk County News</u> Sayville, New York Saturday, March 14, 1891, Page 1, Column 4.

"Town Talk." Bourne buys Course House (Bourne's West Sayville House Fire) <u>Suffolk County News</u> Sayville, New York May 30, 1893, Page 1, Column 2.

"Has He an Enemy?" (Death of Glendale) <u>Suffolk County News</u> Sayville, New York October 21, 1893, Page 1, Column 4.

"Fourth Bay Shor Horse Show Season's Event on South Shore." <u>The Brooklyn Daily Eagle</u> New York July 17, 1904 Page 7.

"Town Talk." (Death of Kenneth) <u>Suffolk County News</u> Sayville, New York December 30, 1898, Page 1, Columns 3 and 4.

"Herold Reporter Lied." (Donovan's Boxing Exhibition) <u>Suffolk County News</u> Sayville, New York July 11, 1913, Page 1, Column 1.

"Many Local Entries for the Horse Show." Brooklyn Daily Eagle New York November 13, 1898, Page 9.

"Old Times." Suffolk County News: Francis Hoag Sayville, New York April 10, 1942, Page 4 (Donovan quote) Baseball Story.

"Romance Behind F.G. Bourne's Gift to Cathedral." The Sun New York, April 19, 1914, Page 6

"Bourne House Burned." The Suffolk County News Sayville, New York August 12, 1893, Page 3.

Untitled: "Town Talk" (Bourne building farm in Oakdale). The Suffolk County News Sayville, New York March 22, 1890, Page 2.

"Big Crops Grown on Long Island." The Brooklyn Daily Eagle Brooklyn, New York October 27, 1901, Page 51.

"Basons to build Bourne's Barns" The Suffolk County News Sayville, New York May 6, 1910, Page 1.

Untitled: "Town Talk" (Bourne Night Watchman foils burglar). The Suffolk County News Sayville, New York January 31, 1908, Page 2.

"F. G. Bourne's $400,000 Villa." The Brooklyn Daily Eagle Brooklyn, New York August 8, 1905, Page 1.

Gary, Christopher. "Once the Tallest Building, but Since 1967 a Ghost." The New York Times, New York Late Edition "East Coast" January 2, 2005.

"Kale Culture at Oakdale" The Brooklyn Daily Eagle Brooklyn, New York July 10, 1902, Page 8.

"$100,000 Stable Burned" <u>The New York Times</u>, New York October 3, 1909, Page 1.

"Bourne's High School Horse Wonder" <u>The Brooklyn Daily Eagle</u> Brooklyn, New York November 12, 1896, Page 12.

"Streetscapes" stories by Christopher Gray <u>The New York Times</u>, New York Various Articles.

Fordyce, James. "Frederick Bourne and Indian Neck Hall" <u>The Long Island Forum</u>, Vol. I, No. 3, March 1987.

ADDITIONAL PHOTOGRAPHS

Many of the homes constructed at Indian Neck were eventually moved to West Street where workers on Bourne's estate lived. These photographs show a house originally on the estate which was moved to West Street and was given to George Metzler and his family (bottom photo). The family later moved further up the block to a larger house previously known as "The Widow Molly Inn."

Another house located at Indian Neck and moved to West Street was the Superintendent's house. When the house was located on West Street (now Dale Drive) it was fondly known as "The Hotel."

One of Frederick Bourne's first automobiles was a 1901 Winton Bullet. The automobile that he most prized were the Daimler Mercedes. Photo courtesy Manhattan College.

Not long after its completion in 1908, the Singer Building was seen by some as a phallic symbol. Greek, Roman and Asian cultures used phallic symbolism in their structures to symbolize fertility. A modern interpretation is of financial and political power. First responders sometimes referred to the tower as

"THE BRICK DICK."

THE DIRECTORS' ROOM

OFFICE FURNITURE

THE Executive Offices of The Singer Manufacturing Company, covering the entire 34th floor of the Singer Building, are equipped throughout with mahogany furniture manufactured by the *Doten-Dunton Desk Co.* of New York and Boston.

The furniture shown in the appended illustration of the Directors' Room is uniform in every detail of design, material, construction and finish, and each piece bears its relation to and architecturally conforms with every other.

It is made throughout of selected Honduras mahogany, and the cabinet work, veneering, carving, etc., is of the highest grade. We mention the following special features:

Drawers, hand dovetailed. Drawer bottoms of three-ply Figured Mahogany. Drawer sides and backs of Figured Mahogany. Solid Division between each two Drawers making separate Dust-proof Compartments. Veneers (except where branch veneers are used) are one quarter inch thick. Branch Veneer panels mitered at center on Davenports, Chairs, Tables and Bookcases.

Such furniture appeals to the discriminating man and creates the right impression upon all who see it.

[74]

Hanging in the Directors Office in the Singer Tower are
portraits of both Frederick Bourne and Isaac Singer.

AN ELECTRIC VENETIAN GONDOLA AT THE THOUSAND ISLANDS

ONE OF THE MORE UNUSUAL vessels constructed for Mr. Bourne was this Electric Venetian Gondola which he and his family used at Dark Island. The forty-foot gondola was built in 1912 in Bayonne, New Jersey. Although powered by electric, the vessel was made according to traditional designs. For instance, the ferri (irons) which decorate the bow and stern are exact reproductions from a boat built in the 11th century and are constructed of polished nickel. Bronze castings of sea horses mounted to teak bases were used for the rowlocks. The electric motor ran on rechargeable storage batteries, giving the vessel the normal speed of 7 ½ miles per hour and a maximum speed of 9 miles per hour. The exterior of the cabin was constructed of hand carved Indian teak and African mahogany. The interior of the felsi (cabin) was luxuriously upholstered in leather. Mr. Bourne originally wished for the gondola to be built in Venice. However, the builders in New Jersey gave the Commodore assurance that they would build it to his satisfaction.

ABOUT THE AUTHOR

AUTHOR PHILIP SELVAGGIO HAS HAD a lifelong love of history. In 1986 Selvaggio moved to New Mexico from his home in Oakdale, New York to learn the science of horseshoeing under the tutelage of world champion farrier and famous western artist Jim Keith. After receiving his certification from the American Farrier's Association, Selvaggio moved back to Oakdale to apply his trade in the New York area. Mr. Selvaggio is also a graduate of SUNY Stony Brook where he majored in English Literature. He currently maintains a residence in Oakdale, New York.

Author Philip Selvaggio
Photograph by Gina Marchese taken at the Bourne Mausoleum,
Greenwood Cemetery Brooklyn, New York

Made in the USA
Las Vegas, NV
02 November 2023

80119066R00085